Alison James is a History Graduate and Showbiz
Journalist who writes about Royals and Celebrities for
the Daily Mail, the Daily Express and Yours magazine.

The Royal Baby Book

*A Heir-Raising History
of all things Royal Baby*

ALISON JAMES

First published in 2013

by Create Space

ISBN-13 : 978-1484054284

Typeset by Charlie Noon

Illustrations by Jenny Phung

For Frank, Charlie, Jenny,
Olivia, Florence and Casper

Contents

Introduction

The birth of every baby is special. It is the most magical, mysterious phenomenon in the human experience. But when that baby is heir - or indeed 'spare' – to the British throne, the world's most famous and distinguished monarchy, it's a whole new realm of magic and mystery altogether. Marry the miracle that is a new life with the rich history of Royalty and you get a kind of double whammy 'Wow' factor – twice the magic, twice the mystery.

Generation after generation have been gripped by fairy and folk tales in which Royal babies have played leading roles. Think 'Sleeping Beauty' where the new-born Princess Aurora is cursed at her christening; 'Rapunzel' in which another new-born Princess is kidnapped for her youth-giving properties; 'Rumpelstiltskin', the story of a tiny baby Prince in danger of being abducted unless his mother can complete the impossible tasks set for her. . . Some of the characters and incidents featured in this book would not be out of place in such mythical stories. In the 1500s, Philip the Handsome, King of Castile, refused to pay for the upkeep of his first child because she was female; Catherine de Medici, a sixteenth century Queen of France, conjured up spells and potions in the hope that she would fall pregnant; Henry, Lord Darnley, second husband of Mary Queen of Scots, forced his heavily pregnant wife to race across Scotland on horseback in the dead of night after the murder of Mary's musician, David Rizzio; and Princess Thyra of Denmark, Edward VII's unmarried sister-in-law, was banished to Greece when she became pregnant by an army officer in 1871 and, having given birth, never again saw her baby who had been immediately handed over to a laundry maid.

Within these pages are tales of hope and fear, joy and pain, drama and conflict, pride and betrayal, triumph and tragedy, life and death, and 'dark' humour, too. Real-life stories played out over the centuries in the history of begetting, carrying and bearing babies of the blood Royal, through to babyhood and beyond. It's a sensational, often surreal, kind of soap opera but one with a sovereign spin. That's not all it is, though. It's also a social history of how we came into being, were born and survived through infancy and childhood. It's the social evolution of these life stages over time from, for example, the Queens of Ancient Egypt who gave birth squatting on two large bricks within a reed-covered dwelling erected specially for childbirth with only amulets and spells spelt out on papyrus to 'ease' labour pain, to today's Royal mothers, some of whom, like the Countess of Wessex, have conceived with the help of IVF techniques.

Where Royalty lead, the rest of us have traditionally tended to follow. The Duchess of Cambridge, like her late mother-in-law, Diana, is the Queen of trendsetters. Catherine's fashion sense, hair and make-up styles are copied the world over – and it's been the same with her maternity wardrobe, how she's conducted her pregnancy, the decisions made regarding the birth of her first infant, and future infants, how she and William choose to raise baby Cambridge, and the names bestowed on the new HRH - the heir to the world's best-known, best-loved monarchy. When Prince Harry was born in September 1984, for instance, his name had never featured on any 'Most Popular' lists yet several years on, it was in the top 10. It was ever thus. Henrietta Maria, wife of seventeenth century King Charles I, was the first woman in the world to give birth assisted by the then top secret gynaecological invention that were forceps; Queen Victoria blazed a child-birthing trail when she became one of the first women in the world to be administered chloroform for pain relief, while her husband Albert was, very unusually for the time, at her bedside on each of the nine occasions she gave birth. Their choice of perambulator - a 'Hitchings' baby carriage with red, white and black livery, and brass fittings – was the must-have purchase for an 1850s yummy mummy, just as Kate Cambridge's 'Bugaboo' pram is for a 2013 one.

The birth of an heir - or spare - affects us all. It is a public event of great importance and symbolic significance. As time goes on, we will get to know this Royal baby so well, it will almost seem as if the new HRH belongs to us all. And just as it is with anyone we know well, we want to know their history, heritage and who came before them. That's just where 'The Royal Baby Book' comes in. . .

I

CONCEPTION
BY ROYAL COMMAND

———

'Everyone asks in a whisper,
The King – can he or can't he?
One says he can't get it up,
Another- he can't get it in!'

Ditty sung around 1770s Versailles when French
King Louis XVI had failed to impregnate Marie
Antoinette after seven years of marriage.

Conceiving a Royal Baby, an heir to the throne, is not all regal 'slap and tickle'. Anything but. If, for instance, Louis XVI had managed to '*get it up*' or '*in*' several years before he finally managed to in 1778, the French Revolution may just have been avoided. Yes really! Childless, bored and frustrated, Marie Antoinette poured all her energies into spending fortunes on outrageously expensive fashions, priceless jewels, hosting obscenely lavish parties, and making-like-a peasant in her 'Petit Trianon' fantasy land within the walls of Versailles. Meanwhile the French people were struggling to buy bread. Impotent Louis indulged Marie Antoinette's every whim and ignored the growing anarchy on 'les rues'. In 1781, having given birth to a '*disappointing*' daughter three years earlier, the Queen finally produced a son and heir but by then it was too late and four years later, 'Vive La Revolution! '

Many a Royal Lady has suffered for conceiving an heir too late or not at all. While a lucky few were married to Kings or Princes who loved them for themselves rather than their fertility, most were regarded as conception commodities. An ovum and a uterus – that's what a Royal Wife was. A Petri-dish for the Royal DNA. This was still apparent as recently as the 1980s when Prince

Charles married Lady Diana Spencer. *'He (Charles) married a womb,'* the Prince's cousin-in-law, Princess Michael of Kent, was quoted as saying in 2005. *'In other words, somebody to give him children.'* If this was true, the late Diana more than did her duty. Within four years of her 1981 marriage, she had conceived, carried and delivered a healthy male heir - and a spare. Royal history would be very different if only Edward the Confessor's Queen, Edith, had done the same.

Did You Know?

Medieval Princesses were often married at an absurdly tender age in order to forge financial and political links with other countries but consummation of a marriage was banned until the young bride had experienced at least two menstrual periods.

MAKING MAJESTIES

In theory, conceiving a Royal child should never have been especially problematic. Peasant or Prince, the process of procreation is the same. Conceiving a son and heir, though, has historically hung over some HRHs' heads like the sword of a reproductively-challenged Damocles. The success of a Royal marriage was measured solely by the protagonists' ability to produce progeny. Fulfilling one's dynastic duty and begetting an heir was all that mattered. Lust, love, mutual respect? Pah! In such circumstances, it's little short of miraculous that certain Royal babies were ever born at all.

Edward Prince of Wales was conceived in January 1453 when his parents, Henry VI and Margaret of Anjou, had been married for eight years. The deeply religious, mentally deranged Henry was said to be '*suspicious of relations*' with his wife, plus the Bishop of Salisbury had urged Henry not to go near

NOT TONIGHT MARGARET

King Henry VI

her. Whether he did or not is debatable - there were rumours the baby Prince was not his father's. While Henry never disowned the boy, he didn't acknowledge the baby's existence for the first 18 months of his life.

Edward VI was conceived in January 1537 but his father Henry VIII admitted, three months after marrying Jane Seymour in May 1536, that '*he felt himself already growing old and doubted whether he should have any child by the Queen.*' Henry may well have had problems with his own fertility but, typical tyrant, he blamed Jane for failing to fall pregnant quickly. He 'punished' her by not getting her crowned.

Louis IV of France. Conceived in 1637, the future 'Sun King's' mother, Anne of Austria, discovered she was expecting him after 22 years of marriage to his father, Louis XIII. She'd suffered a number of still births early in the marriage but hadn't slept with her estranged husband for years. Then one stormy night, in December 1637, Louis was unable to travel, had a few drinks and ended up in his wife's bed. One night was enough. When baby Louis was born nine months later, the official newspaper 'Gazette de France' proclaimed it '*a marvel when it was least expected*'.

George II. Conceived in January 1683, his parents, the future George I and Sophia Dorothea of Celle, hated each others' guts. When it was first proposed that the stunning Sophia marry her dimwit of a cousin she flung his portrait across the room, screeching, *'I will not marry the pig-snout!'* Marry the pig-snout she did, though, and it was a match made in Royal hell. George had servants spy on Sophia and flaunted his ugly mistress, known as the 'Ogress', in front of her. Sophia, meanwhile, shredded his personality – or lack of it – in public. Somehow George and Sophia did manage to conceive young George (and a daughter three years later) but when Sophia had an affair in 1689, her husband tried to choke her to death. When that failed, he vowed never to see her again, banned any further mention of her and had her placed under house arrest in Hanover for the rest of her life – some 31 long years.

Queen Victoria. Conceived in August 1818 during what was known as *'Hymen's War Terrific'* (the race between the middle-aged sons of the ailing George III to begat themselves a legitimate heir), Victoria's father, the 51-year-old Duke of Kent, had never fathered a child although he'd been living with his mistress, the exotically-named French-Canadian former prostitute,

Julie de St Laurent, for nearly 30 years. Yet within a few months of marrying Victoire, the Dowager Princess of Leiningen, the Duke had made her pregnant. Either Victoire was exceptionally fertile, Julie was infertile or. . . the Duke wasn't Victoria's father!

Prince Harry was conceived at Sandringham over Christmas 1983, with the late Princess Diana likening the conception to a miracle as she and Prince Charles had stopped sharing a bed by then. *'I don't know how my husband and I did have Harry because by then he (Charles) had gone back to his lady (Camilla) but. . . one thing that is absolutely sure is that we did.'*

Did You Know?

Elizabeth I's parents married only after she had been conceived. Henry VIII and Anne Boleyn secretly wed in January 1533, Elizabeth having been conceived at the beginning of December 1532.

Honeymoon Conceptions

Royal Honeymoons have, historically speaking, always been rather more complex than the usual post-nuptial vacation. As always with Royalty, it was about conceiving an heir as quickly as possible but certain courtly customs and conditions hardly encouraged speedy conception. Until the 1750s, the public 'putting-to-bed' of Royal newly-weds was as much a part of the celebrations as cutting the cake. At most of these weddings the guests would only depart once the bride and groom had been officially bedded - that is, they'd been partially undressed and climbed in beneath the coverlets. But occasionally even then the couple still wouldn't be left alone. On the wedding night of the future Mary II and her cousin William of Orange in 1677, their uncle, Charles II, was heard shouting through the door, '*Now nephew to your work! Hey! St George for England!*' Some Royal newly-weds were even forced to 'perform' before an audience. When Catherine de Medici married Prince Henri of France in 1533, her voyeuristic father-in-law, King Francis, remained in the bridal suite until the deed was seen to have been done. '*I wished to watch them jousting,*' he said, '*and each showed valour in the joust.*' After such a disturbing experience, perhaps it's not surprising

Catherine didn't conceive for another 10 years. Some Royal newly-weds have done as bidden, though, and conceived a child within weeks of marriage.

Prince Arthur of Wales. Henry VIII's elder brother was born a few weeks prematurely in Winchester on September 20 1486, some eight months after the Westminster wedding of his parents, Lancastrian Henry VII and Elizabeth of York, and a year after Henry had ascended the throne. The new daddy must have been delirious with relief as the Tudors claim to the throne was decidedly shaky. The canny King played a PR blinder and named his son after the legendary King Arthur from whom Henry claimed the Tudors were descended.

Princess Charlotte. Conceived in April 1795, Charlotte's father, the future George IV, was disgusted by her *'never well washed'* mother, Caroline of Brunswick. He spent most of their wedding night collapsed in a drunken heap with his head in the fireplace. But he did do his duty and steeled himself to have with sex with Caroline – but on just three occasions. *'I have known her three times – twice the first and once the second night – it required no small effort to conquer my aversion and overcome the disgust* *of her person,'* the Prince told an aide. *'There were such marks of filth both in the fore and hind part of her and I made a vow never to touch her again.'* Fortunately George, also known as 'Prinny', managed to make Caroline pregnant during one of those three drunken honeymoon 'performances'. Caroline was more surprised than anyone and made it known she had not thought her husband up to it. Prinny never forgave her for the slight on his virility.

Princess Victoria. The first child of Prince Albert and Queen Victoria was conceived on their honeymoon in early Spring 1840. At least she would have been if her parents had taken a honeymoon. While Albert had expressed a wish not to *'depart from the usual custom in England for married people to stay up to four or six weeks from the town and society'*, his workaholic wife, who was also his Queen, refused to take more than two days off. *'Dearest,'* she wrote to him. *'I am the Sovereign and that business can stop and wait for nothing'*. But neither could the baby-making. Within a few weeks of their marriage, Victoria discovered she was pregnant, declaring it *'too dreadful'*.

Princess Caroline of Monaco was born nine months and four days after the wedding of Prince Rainier and

sea or morning sickness?

princess Grace of Monaco

Princess Grace, which had taken place in April 1956. Caroline was conceived in the diamond and ruby-encrusted Master Suite of the 'Deo Juvante II', the 147 foot yacht which Greek shipping magnate Aristotle Onassis had given her parents as a wedding present. The newly-weds cruised around the Mediterranean for several weeks before returning to Monaco where the pregnancy was confirmed. That should have been a given - former film star Grace had been subject to a fertility test before the wedding.

Prince William of Wales was conceived in October 1981 when his parents were on the Balmoral leg of their extended honeymoon. Diana famously hated staying on the Scottish estate but at least one good thing came of it. William's conception was, said Diana, '*A godsend.*

It was marvellous news that occupied my mind. Thank heavens for William.'

Did You Know?

Henrietta Maria, Queen of Charles I, was described as 'barren' when she still hadn't conceived after four years of marriage. But it was down to the fact that her husband was spending all his time with his beloved favourite, the Duke of Buckingham. Once the Buck 'buck' had been murdered in 1628, grieving Charles finally sought out his wife and she fell pregnant within a few months.

—

DESPERATE MEASURES

Historically, contraception has never been a matter to occupy a Royal Wife. The aim was to conceive as many children as possible. This was one of the reasons a newborn would be placed with a wet-nurse as soon as he or she emerged from the Regal birth canal - breastfeeding delayed ovulation and therefore the conception of another child. Marie of Romania, a grand daughter of Queen Victoria, was forbidden by her husband's uncle, King Carol I, to breastfeed after she'd given birth to her first child in October 1893, although she pleaded to do so. Having proved her fertility, she was made to hop straight back into the marital bed, conceive again and become a kind of child-bearing conveyor belt. Conception of a son and heir eluded other Royal Wives - unfortunate for their, usually adoptive, country but potentially disastrous for them. The outlook wasn't good for a Royal Wife who couldn't conceive. If she really was little more than a womb to her husband, she may as well not exist – or at least be sent back from whence she came, a 'barren' embarrassment to all. The fact that any fertility fault might be the male's was rarely considered. Misogyny ruled! If the Royal Sire had proved his potency by fathering illegitimate offspring, humiliation was heaped upon humiliation. Little wonder, then, some Royal Ladies took truly desperate measures in order to try and get themselves in the family way.

Catherine de Medici. Italian-born Catherine married the future French King, Henri II, in October 1533 when both were hormonally-charged 14-year -olds, yet a decade on, she still had not conceived a child. Henri did his wedding-night duty but then pointedly avoided his wife. He was in love with Cougar-like lady of the court, Diane de Poitiers, who was twice his age. It was with her that Henri spent his nights although, ever the pragmatist, Diane would send him to Catherine once he'd made love to her. Catherine still failed to conceive and, in desperation, had two small holes drilled into the floor of her chamber so she could spy on Henri and Diane in the room below. This voyeurism backfired, however, with Catherine tearfully reporting that the husband she adored had *never used her so well.* In desperation, she experimented with alchemy, tarot and spells in the hope of boosting her fertility, and tried every quack remedy going – including gulping down gallon after gallon of mule's urine and placing upon her *source of life*, ie, her vagina, a stinking poultice made from mare's milk, ground stag's antlers and cow dung. As the Venetian Ambassador rightly observed, *From this I would deduce she is more at risk of increasing her difficulty rather than finding the solution.* Eventually a doctor examined Catherine and Henri, and discovered both had slight physical abnormalities. Her womb was inverted, while he had a common condition known as 'chordee', a downward curve of the penis. Catherine was advised that they should start practising sex 'a levrette', une levrette being a female greyhound. It was good advice. Within a few months of Catherine turning her back on her husband, she finally became pregnant.

Marie Antoinette. France's tragic Queen wasn't exactly proactive about the non-consummation of her marriage and therefore the non-conception of an heir. She preferred to vent her frustration in letters home to Austria rather than taking up the matter with husband, Louis. Seven years after the marriage, Marie Antoinette's brother, the Emperor Joseph, was dispatched to Paris as a kind of Imperialist sex therapist. A highly embarrassed Marie Antoinette finally admitted to her big brother that *'in bed he (Louis) has good hard erections. The organ remains there motionless for two minutes or so, then withdraws, still stiff without discharging. He says he does it out of duty and without the slightest enjoyment. It makes no sense as from time to time he has night-time ejaculations.'* Joseph wrote in a letter to his brother Leopold that *'(Louis) needs to be beaten like an ass to make him discharge his spunk'* but he addressed his sister rather more delicately, advising her to *'be tender, be warm, above all be patient – get him to bed with you in the afternoon before he is sunk into a state of apathy'.* The big brotherly advice yielded results. A few weeks after Joseph's visit in summer 1777, Marie Antoinette sent a letter home stating that *'more than a week ago my marriage was thoroughly consummated.'* Six months later, she had conceived her first child.

Catherine of Braganza. Charles II's many mistresses were constantly conceiving so why did his wife only manage to fall pregnant once? It wasn't because her philandering husband was too busy elsewhere. Sex addict Charles was more than happy to try and impregnate his little Portuguese wife in addition to practically every other woman at court. As Catherine's fertility – or lack of – was savagely gossiped about, she regularly visited the spas at Tunbridge Wells and Bath, hoping the waters would increase her fertility. She even resorted to placing live pigeons at her feet when she was in bed, an old wives' tale said to increase the changes of conception! This didn't work and can hardly have inflamed Charles' ardour, either. The years went by and the King could have had the marriage

PIGEON-TOED

princess of Braganza

annulled but he chose not to, possibly because long-suffering Catherine put up with his relentless philandering.

Catherine the Great of Russia. After seven years of marriage to Grand Duke Peter, heir to the Russian throne, the stunningly beautiful 16-year-old Catherine was still a virgin – and so was he. The problem, or one of them, was that the severely infantile Peter preferred playing with his toy soldiers or his dolls to making love to his wife – or any other woman for that matter. When Peter had spent an evening publicly hanging a rat for daring to nibble his precious soldiers, his matriarchal aunt, the Empress Elizabeth, decided something must be done. She insisted the couple immediately be instructed in the facts of life while hinting that Catherine should try and get pregnant by any means and any man! Peter's chamberlain Sergei Saltykov didn't need much encouragement. Catherine fell for him immediately, declaring '*he was as handsome as the dawn*'. It's not known for sure whether Sergei or Peter, who was eventually cajoled into copulating with his wife, impregnated Catherine but as her son, Prince Paul, grew up with Peter's unfortunate looks, it seems likely that the child was indeed the Grand Duke's.

Queen Elizabeth, the Queen Mother. When, after two years of marriage to the future George VI, Elizabeth, the then Duchess of York, had still not conceived, it was rumoured within certain circles that, on the advice of her gynaecologist, Elizabeth was artificially inseminated with her husband's sperm. If so, she was not the first Royal Lady to have used the 'turkey baster' method of conception. In May 1461 Princess Juana of Portugal was impregnated by means of a primitive pump device containing the '*watery*' sperm of her impotent husband, Enrique IV of Castile. Or was she? Her daughter, born nine months later, was nicknamed 'la Beltraneja' because she bore more than a passing resemblance to a handsome courtier named Beltran de la Cueva.

Did You Know?

When beautiful Eleanor of Aquitaine married her first husband, Louis VII of France, in 1137, it was expected she would conceive an heir in record time. Louis, however, was deeply religious and, in accordance with Church rules of the time, refused to share his wife's bed on Sundays, Feast days, Saints' days, during Lent and whenever she had her period. Even when he did sleep with her, the Church forbade certain sexual positions and the use of aphrodisiacs. '*I thought I had married a King but I find I have married a monk,*' she lamented. After seven long years, Eleanor finally conceived a daughter, and then another, but once she had laid eyes on the future Henry II and his brooding brand of medieval machismo, she divorced Louis and married the English King.

A Recipe for Royal Fertility

We'll refrain from listing the methodology of Catherine de Medici's mare's milk and cow dung vaginal poultice but she may well have cast this rather more fragrant spell upon herself.

Botanical Fertility Spell

Hollow out the inside of a vulva-shaped candle. Stuff it full of a selection of basic botanicals of fertility – these include snake roots, black-eyed peas, corn, figs, jasmine, lilies, lotuses, melons, moonflowers, mugwort, assorted nuts, olives, pomegranates, poppies, pumpkins, roses and wheat. Use leaves, flowers or seeds rather than the fruit or vegetable itself. Then burn the candle – and let nature take its course. . .

Did You Know?

In 1571 Marfa Vasilevna Sobakina, the third wife of sixteenth century Russian Tsar 'Ivan the Terrible', died as the result of taking a fertility potion administered by her own mother.

AGE MATTERS

In the past, the primary concern of a Royal marriage was to conceive as many babies as possible so as soon as a Princess was capable of conceiving, she would be set to the task for which she had been born. Some started young, very young, but what is surprising is that other Royal Ladies carried on conceiving well into their 40s which, in medieval terms when only a few well-born women managed to live beyond their 50s, was practically geriatric. Fast forward a few hundred years and young Royal Wives were getting pregnant while their twenty first century contemporaries are still at school. Fast forward another 350 years and the matter of conception has become a scientific phenomenon.

12

Margaret Beaufort was little more than a child herself when she conceived the future Henry VII in April 1456. This was considered too young even by late medieval standards and Margaret was shunned during her pregnancy.

14

Mary de Bohun married the future Henry IV in 1380 when she was 12 and he was 13. Henry's father,

John of Gaunt, ordered that the marriage remain unconsummated until Mary was 16 but the couple disobeyed, with the result that she became pregnant at 14.

15

The future **Queen Mary II** was pregnant within a few months of her 1677 marriage to first cousin, Prince William of Orange, but she suffered a miscarriage following a bone-jolting carriage ride across northern Europe. She suffered two further miscarriages and never did give her husband – or her country - an heir.

40

Constance of Hautville, Queen of Sicily and Germany, conceived her first child in 1194 aged 40. Until this point she'd been known as 'The Barren Queen'.

43 (almost)

Sophie Countess of Wessex gave birth to her second child James, Viscount Seven, in December 2007 just weeks before her 43rd birthday. A true blessing, she conceived him naturally even though she had undergone IVF treatment in order to conceive his elder

Sophie, Duchess of Wessex

I AM 43

sister, Lady Louise Windsor, four years earlier.

44

Eleanor of Aquitane's 11th and final child, the future King John, was conceived in March 1166 when she was well into her 40s. But this was no ordinary woman – at 78 years of age, she rode across the Pyrenees on horseback.

51

Johanna of Pfirt, the mother of *Duke Leopold III of Austria,* was 51 when he was born on November 1 1351. He was her sixth surviving child but sadly she died when he was just two-weeks-old.

60

We use the term 'Royal' loosely here but the self-styled *Princess Paul of Romania* certainly considers herself to be blue-blooded, courtesy of her marriage to Prince Paul, pretender to the Romanian throne. Detroit-born Leia Triff as was, gave birth to Prince Carol Ferdinand in Bucharest in January 2010. *'He's a little miracle,'* she said afterwards. *'We were blessed by fine doctors, here in Romania, in the US and in Harley Street in London.'* Leia maintains her child is the product of one of her own frozen eggs. Hmmmm. . .

Did You Know?

It's rumoured that before his 1973 marriage to Princess Anne, Captain Mark Phillips was ordered to provide a specimen of sperm. When its potency was assured, the Queen is supposed to have offered him a title – which he respectfully declined!

—

INCONCEIVABLE

What of the Royal Wives who never managed to conceive a child? Those who were tagged 'barren' – surely one of the bleakest words in the English language? The religious view was that a woman's, and therefore a Queen's, 'barrenness' was symbolic of life itself. To be barren was some kind of punishment, yet it also states in the Bible that if a nation was obedient and pious there would be no 'barren' women amongst the population. Women who did God's will would be blessed with children. Er, not always. Some childless Queens were so often at prayer, it's a wonder they ever found time to do their conjugal 'duty'. *'Get thee to a Nunnery'* was no empty threat for some pre-1066 and medieval Royal Wives unable to conceive. But a number of Royal Wives may have been relieved to step away from the male-dominated, conception-obsessed court. A nunnery or convent offered women a rare taste of freedom. It was one of the very few places where they, rather than men, held positions of power. A childless, Royal ex-wife could devote herself to prayer, indulge in embroidery and spinning, maybe even illustrate a religious manuscript or two. For other ex-wives, though, a convent proved to be claustrophobic. After a period in isolation, they hung up their habits, rejoined the world, married again and finally conceived children.

Judith Queen of Wessex. Married at the tender age of 12 to 46-year-old Ethelwulf King of Wessex in 856, by 858 Judith was a widow and it's doubtful the marriage was ever consummated. She then married 24-year-old Ethelbald, Ethelwulf's son from his first marriage, who didn't think it mattered that he was marrying his step-mother who was 10 years his junior. It mattered to the all powerful Church, however. The marriage was eventually annulled in 860 on the grounds of consanguinity, meaning the pair was too closely related even though there was no blood link between them. Judith, twice a Queen by the time she was 16, was sent to a nunnery on her father's orders. However she eloped with a nobleman called Baldwin and went on to have four children.

Queen Elgifu. Lover and briefly the Queen of King Edwy the Fair who angered his advisors by preferring Elgifu's bed chamber to the council chamber. Elgifu, denounced as a *'strumpet'* by St Dunstan, was the daughter of her husband's former mistress, also named Elgifu – the King is said to have cavorted *'shamelessly'* and *'alternatively'* with both mother and daughter the day after his coronation. The marriage was annulled in 958 as Edwy and Elgifu the Younger were third cousins and thought to be too closely related. Interestingly, this is the same degree of consanguinity as exists between Queen Elizabeth II and Prince Philip.

Queen Edith. Lady Edith Godwin of Wessex was married to Edward the Confessor from 1045 to 1066 but she never conceived. No wonder if, as has been claimed, Edward was really a monk in King's clothing and had taken a vow of celibacy. Whether he had or not, husband and wife were not always on the best terms. Edward had periods of despising his in-laws, expelling them from the country while he packed Edith off to a nunnery. But the stand-off only lasted a year. By 1052, the Godwins were back at court. So was Edith – but not in her husband's bed.

Queen Adeliza was 18 when she married the 53-year-old Henry I in 1121. He had been married before but lost his son and heir, William, in a disaster at sea. He had several illegitimate sons but longed for a legitimate heir. The marriage was consummated but Adeliza did not conceive. In desperation she wrote to the Archbishop of Tours and received the following reply: '*Perhaps the Lord has closed up your womb so that you might adopt immortal offspring. It is more blessed to be fertile in the spirit than the flesh*'. Her flesh, however, was fully operational when, after Henry's death, Adeliza married again – after the obligatory stay in a nunnery, that is. She and her second husband had seven children.

Berengaria. Why didn't Richard I's Spanish wife conceive? The fact that they hardly ever saw each other might have had something to do with it. Apart from one brief spell when she joined him on crusade, throughout their eight year marriage they were never in the same country at the same time – let alone the same bed. Thought to have been gay, the bottom line is that Richard probably preferred a different kind of Queen.

Isabella of Gloucester. She was a Countess in her own right when she married the future King John in

1189 but the Pope forbade sexual relations between the two as they were related – second cousins to be exact. John spent the next 10 years fathering illegitimate children while Isabella spent from the Royal coffers. Once he became King in 1199, John had their marriage annulled but seems it was an amicable split. Isabella let her ex keep the land she had originally brought to the marriage.

Anne of Bohemia. Richard II loved his Bohemian Queen. Married in 1382, they were rarely separated and were said to be remarkably intimate. Anne, however, failed to conceive – possibly because religious Richard had declared himself celibate, emulating his predecessor, Edward the Confessor, whom he greatly admired. He was '*wild with grief*' when she died of the plague aged just 24 in 1394. When he died some 16 years later, they were buried together as Richard had requested. Their joint tomb in Westminster Abbey is damaged but originally showed them clasping hands.

Isabella of France was shipped to England in 1396 when widower Richard II decided to marry again and try to conceive an heir. He was in no hurry, though, as his new wife was only seven! The marriage was (thankfully) never consummated and Richard treated

Isabella like the daughter he had never had. Richard was overthrown and imprisoned by Henry Bolingbroke, the future Henry IV in 1399, who decided the 10-year-old Isabella should marry his son, the future Henry V of England. Brave Isabella refused. Once she knew her husband was dead in early 1400, she went into mourning and eventually the new King gave her permission to return to France where she went on to marry a nobleman and gave birth to a daughter.

Anne of Cleves. A disastrous coupling from the off, Henry VIII christened his fourth wife 'The Flanders Mare' when she arrived in England in late 1539, declaring that '*he liked her not*'. But Anne must have been massively underwhelmed, too. She had been expecting '*the most handsome prince in Christendom*' but found instead an obese, middle-aged man with a foul-smelling, ulcerated leg. The wedding night proved to be a revelation – but not in a good way - with Henry later saying '*Never could I be provoked to know her carnally.*' Ironically, the wedding bed was engraved with a male cherub brandishing an enormous erection and a female version boasting a belly big with child. Henry visited his doctors, telling them his new wife was '*still as good as a maid*'. His own virility, he claimed, was not in question as he had made a number of '*nocturnal emissions*' during this time. Not wishing to nocturnally emit with Anne, Henry had the marriage annulled on the grounds of non-consummation. Anne became the King's '*Dear Sister*' and lived out the rest of her days in the palaces she had received as part of her divorce settlement.

Katherine Howard. Henry adored his fifth wife, the nubile, sexually precocious Katherine, whom he married in July 1540. It was love at first sight for the 50-year-old King while Katherine, 19, was intoxicated with the kudos that came with being Queen. But she did not conceive. Henry may well have been impotent by this time but it's also been mooted that Katherine could have been infertile, due to a crude form of contraception, recommended to her, bizarrely enough, by her step grandmother, several years earlier. The Dowager Duchess of Norfolk had raised Katherine but had been somewhat lax. Katherine lost her virginity at just 14 to her music teacher who had pounced on her while she was practicing on the virginals! More lovers followed and it's rumoured the Duchess instructed Katherine to insert coins into her vagina in order to block the entrance to her cervix. This may have led to an infection which made her infertile. Ultimately it hardly mattered. Katherine's pre-marital dalliances came to light, ditto her extra marital affair with Thomas Culpepper, and Henry had his *'rose without a thorn'* beheaded less than two years after he'd married her.

Katherine Howard

Katherine Parr. Twice widowed by the time she married Henry in July 1543, the King was now well and truly impotent, and as wide as he was tall. More nursemaid and companion than wife in the Biblical sense, Katherine outlived Henry and, once widowed, lost no time in marrying Thomas Seymour, the late Jane's brother and the man she had fallen in love with before Henry had virtually commanded her to marry him. Thomas made the dowager Queen pregnant within seven months of their secret May 1547 wedding. She gave birth on August 30 1548 but sadly died four days later.

Queen Mary. 'Bloody Mary' as she was dubbed, ascended the throne in 1553 and was truly desperate to conceive an heir with Philip of Spain, the husband with whom she was besotted. But there was a problem – or three. At 38, her fertility was on the wane; Philip wasn't attracted to her, *'The Queen is not pretty. . .she dresses very badly'*; plus she had suffered from gynaecological problems all her adult life. On two separate occasions as her *'belly grew big'*, she was convinced she was pregnant but it was a combination of wishful thinking and existing health issues.

Amalia of Oldenburg was a German princess who became a Greek Queen but she never gave her husband an heir. A post-mortem carried out after her death, aged 57 in 1875, revealed she had neither uterus nor fallopian tubes.

The Duchess of Windsor. Rumours abound as to why the thrice married Wallis never conceived a baby with her *'Dook'*, as she called the former Edward VIII. She was a hermaphrodite; she was really a man;

she had (according to British Intelligence) *'genitalia knotted like grapes'* that prevented intercourse... There seems, however, to have been a far less sensational reason for her inability to conceive. According to her personal physician, the Duchess had *'normal female sexual organs'* but in the early 1930s had also had a hysterectomy.

Did You Know?

Elizabeth I was famously known as the Virgin Queen yet during her lifetime it was rumoured that she had, in fact, conceived one child and possibly more – a miscarried daughter while she was still a Princess by her stepmother's husband, Thomas Seymour, and a secret son by her favourite Robert Dudley's child once she became Queen.

IMPOTENT POTENTATES

Few Kings have admitted their inability to rule in the bedchamber. To do so would have been seen as a weakness and left them open to ridicule – like Louis XVI and that *'Can he/Can't he?'* riddle. If a King was impotent, the same would be said of his power as a Monarch. Most vitally it meant he couldn't produce an heir and ensure succession so it was nearly always their wives who were blamed for being infertile. A King's virility was not called into dispute until it became impossible to ignore. A whispered aside to an intimate at Court would soon become common knowledge. While impotency was for some potentates, a temporary malfunction, for others it was a more permanent state of affairs. . .

Henry VIII. His bulk can hardly have helped his virility but his 'men's problem' was in evidence even before he became an incredible hulk. It seems likely that Anne Boleyn, his second wife, told her sister-in-law, Jane Boleyn, that Henry had difficulty in sustaining an erection and the news got out. This dysfunction has been linked to syphilis but it's more likely Henry was suffering from type two diabetes which can also be a cause of male impotence. Henry, it seems, did have rather an inferiority complex about his virility and was guilty of doing the Tudor equivalent of stuffing a pair of socks down his briefs in order to inflate his manhood. He padded his codpiece, causing a trend of larger and larger 'pieces', which did not fall out of fashion until the end of the sixteenth century.

Henri II of France. Despite the 'chordee', he performed without difficulty with his mistress Diane de Poitier plus he impregnated the sister of his groom after just one night. So strictly speaking, he wasn't incapable. Sad to say but it sounds like his wife was the problem – he just wasn't attracted to Catherine and could only have sex with her in the 'greyhound' way when he didn't have to look at her!

Louis XVI. His phimosis (too-tight foreskin) made intercourse extremely painful and he told his grandfather, King Louis XV, a year after his marriage to Marie Antoinette that he had *'attempted to consummate his marriage but feelings of pain always prevented him from doing so, and he was uncertain whether the pain was caused by a physical abnormality.'* Hardly a man of action, it was another six years before Louis had sex with his wife - after Louis had either finally agreed to a circumcision or long-dormant passions had finally come to life. Although he spoke of his *'great pleasure'*, the truth is that he simply was not highly sexed – he was the only French 'Louis' never to have a mistress.

Grand Duke Peter of Russia. Could be the Grand Duke also suffered from a phimosis but his problem was a mental one, too – as his long suffering wife Catherine attested as she listened to him scraping at his violin and thrashing his dogs each night. *'I admit that I was driven half mad and suffered terribly as both these performances tore at my ear drums. . . After the dogs I was the most miserable creature in the world.'*

Ferdinand I of Austria. As a result of his parents' genetic closeness (they were double first cousins), Ferdinand, born April 19 1793, suffered from epilepsy, hydrocephalus, neurological problems, a speech impediment and was therefore, not surprisingly, incapable of consummating his marriage to Maria Anna of Sardinia.

Napoleon. Not exactly well-endowed in the 'pantalon' department, even his wife Josephine was known to mutter *'Bon-a-parte, c'est bon a rien'* – *'Bonaparte is good for nothing'*. In fact, his body was in some ways more like a woman's than a man's but bizarrely he was proud of his cleavage, boasting, *'More than one beautiful woman would glory in a chest like mine.'* He didn't father a child until his late 30s.

Edward VIII, Duke of Windsor. Wife Wallis wittily quipped he wasn't *'heir-conditioned'* and according to a FBI report, a minor German royal with connections to the Royal Family, revealed the Duchess had told guests at a Paris party that, *'The duke is impotent and although he had tried sexual intercourse with numerous women, they had all been unsuccessful in satisfying his passions.'* Could this be why he was known by many as *'The Little Prince'*?

"The Dook is not heir – conditioned"

Wallis Simpson

Did You Know?

Ferdinand of Aragon, Katherine of Aragon's father, attempted to boost his fertility by feasting on bull's testicles. Not that he needed to 'up' his sperm count – he fathered five legitimate and four illegitimate children. But maybe that was all down to the bulls' balls.

—

CAST ASIDE

So the nunnery was the time-honoured dumping ground for Royal Wives who could neither conceive nor produce the required son and heir. In a world where the Roman Church was all powerful, Royal marriages would be annulled on various, often tenuous, grounds trumped up by His Holiness the Pope, leaving a King free to marry again and hopefully sew his seed on more fertile ground. Powerless against the might of the church and their husbands' will, discarded Royal Wives would go quietly - at least they did until Henry VIII tried to dispose of his first wife in the 1520s.

Catherine of Aragon could conceive for England, and indeed her native Spain, but she ran out of luck when it came to carrying full term or giving birth to live and/or healthy babies. She conceived at least seven times yet the future Mary I was the only child of Catherine and Henry's marriage. Once Catherine started going through the menopause in the mid 1520s, the writing was on the oak-panelled wall but how could Henry rid himself of the loyal wife he had been married to for so many years? A Bible passage from the book of Leviticus came to his rescue – '*And if a man shall take his brother's wife, it is an unclean thing: they shall be childless*'. Before she wed Henry in 1509, Catherine had been married to his elder brother, Prince Arthur, who died six months after their wedding in 1502, and although Henry and Catherine had a daughter, as far as Henry was concerned, a mere girl counted for nothing. Henry approached Pope Clement VII with a view to getting the marriage annulled. The idea was that Catherine would then enter a nunnery, leaving Henry free to marry again and sire several healthy sons. But it didn't work out like that. Swearing she had never had sex with Arthur, Catherine refused to comply. Unusually the Pope sided with her, no doubt because he was in the camp of Catherine's nephew, Emperor Charles V. Henry was stuck and under increasing pressure from his would-be-wife Anne Boleyn to act. The 'King's Great Matter' dragged on for the next six years. When Catherine refused to do Henry's will, he refused to let her see their daughter and, more-or-less, left her to rot in a succession of draughty castles. Finally, he broke with Rome, declared himself Head of the English Church and married Anne in early 1533. Catherine, vowing she was Henry's wife to the end, died three years later.

Anne Boleyn. Arguably history's most famous discarded Royal wife, Anne, like Catherine before her, had no problems conceiving. In addition to daughter Elizabeth born on September 7 1533, she conceived on two further occasions but miscarried the babies – both of whom were boys. Henry wasn't sympathetic, brutally telling Anne after the second miscarriage '*that he would have no more boys by her*'. Having turned the Kingdom upside down just a few years earlier in order to free himself of his first wife, he could hardly now divorce his second – especially as he had no grounds. His 'yes-men' most likely fabricated infidelities on Anne's part which Henry was more than happy to believe. She was accused of committing adultery with five men, one of whom was her own brother. She was found guilty and executed in May 1536.

Empress Josephine. She had no trouble conceiving two children during her first marriage but although Napoleon was obsessed with Josephine *'the pleasure and torment of his life'*, she could not conceive a baby with him. He would mock her about this from time to time, saying that women were *'mere baby making machines'*, but it was common knowledge that Napoleon was not exactly well-endowed and neither had he made any of his myriad mistresses pregnant. Until, that is, in 1807, the 20-year-old Marie Waleska discovered she was *'enceinte'*. Divorce was staring Josephine, now a menopausal 44, in the face but Napoleon could not bring himself to discuss it with her – he would be physically ill whenever the subject came up. Finally one of Napoleon's ministers broke the news. The interests of France, Josephine was told, demanded the Emperor choose a fertile womb over marital contentment. Josephine was devastated and her distraught sobbing could be heard throughout the Palace of Fontainebleau. Napoleon said he pitied her but had not been prepared for her *'outburst of grief'*. Just what was he expecting after 13 years of marriage? On January 10th 1810, Napoleon and Josephine were divorced in a candlelit ceremony in the throne room at Fontainebleau. Both were in tears. Napoleon was at least generous to the woman he had discarded because she hadn't fallen pregnant – he paid off her debts, gave her a lavish annual allowance and let her keep the Elysee Palace as her Parisian residence. She also kept her country house and all her jewels. Napoleon did finally get himself an heir, courtesy of Marie-Louise of Austria, but Josephine never stopped loving him.

Empress Josephine

When he was exiled to the Mediterrean island of Elba in 1814, she declared that if '*it were not for his wife I would go lock myself up with him*'. Ironically the Royal Houses of Denmark, Sweden, Luxembourg, Belgium, Norway and Greece are all descended from Josephine via her son and daughter from her first marriage which ended after 15 unhappy years when husband Alexandre de Beauharnais was guillotined in 1794.

Princess Soraya of Iran. The Shah of Iran married his second wife in 1951 but by 1958 the marriage was in trouble due to Soraya's inability to conceive – she had travelled to Europe for fertility treatment but to no avail. The Shah was advised to either take another wife in addition to Soraya or divorce her. Soraya refused to be usurped so the couple divorced. The 25-year-old Queen said it was '*a sacrifice of my own happiness*'.

Did You Know?

There is a brand of contraception pill in the USA marketed as the 'Camilla'.

II

' WE' ARE
EXPECTING

———

'Look how her figure is swelling!'

The Emperor Napoleon proudly showing off his
second wife, the pregnant Marie Louise of Austria, to
Hortense, the daughter of his first wife, Josephine.

The arrival of Baby Cambridge brings a change in the order of succession while also preserving the continuation of an ancient Royal line. For the Royal Lady carrying a precious new life within her body, there has, historically speaking, always been extra pressure in addition to the usual stresses and strains of pregnancy. Napoleon may well have been proud of his pregnant young wife but this was a man who announced that *women are nothing but machines for producing children*. This dubious philosophy was even more pertinent for a Royal Lady who may well have been carrying the future of a dynasty around in her womb. There was the worry, or in some instances, fear, that the baby would turn out to be a girl instead of the longed-for boy. It is also only in relatively recent times that a substantial percentage of Royal pregnancies hasn't ended in miscarriage or still birth. As we're celebrating the arrival of the new baby Cambridge, we will not dwell on such misfortune. Instead let's take a look at how pregnancy has impacted on Royals throughout the ages.

Did You Know?

George III's Queen, Charlotte, was pregnant for a total of 22 years, from 1761 to 1783. Not one of these 15 pregnancies ended in miscarriage or stillbirth and 13 of the children reached adulthood.

TESTING, TESTING. . .

The signs and symptoms of pregnancy are timeless –
the cessation of menstruation, tender breasts, possible
sickness and, later in the pregnancy, feeling the baby
move. This last symptom, known as *'quickening'*, was
the ultimate sure sign of pregnancy for centuries.
But, given that pregnancy has had such significance
for Royals, it is highly likely that, throughout history,
other methods were employed to try and find out
if a blue-blooded baby was on the way. Catherine,
Duchess of Cambridge, no doubt 'pee'd on a stick' in
the privacy of her own 'throne room' to discover if she
was pregnant but it never used to be so easy, quick nor
simple. So just how might Royal Ladies throughout
history have discovered that they were, er, regally
'knocked up'?

The Queens of Ancient Egypt would have urinated on
the germinated grains of barley and emmer wheat to
find out if they were pregnant. If the barley sprouted
first, it was thought the child would be male but if
the emmer did, the child would be female. If neither
sprouted then the Royal Lady was not pregnant.
Testings done in 1963 showed there was some credence
to this theory. In 70% of instances, the urine of

pregnant women caused the seeds to grow. Researchers suspect the Ancient Egyptians were probably the first civilization to detect a change in the urine of a pregnant woman, even if they did not understand about hormones and oestrogen levels as we do today. Another method employed in Ancient Egypt was for a potentially expectant woman to place an onion bulb deep within her vagina overnight. Detecting the smell of the onion on the woman's breath the next morning was a sign that she was pregnant. It is thought that this 'onion breath' was due to absorption of the vegetable's sulphuric compounds into the woman's blood via engorged blood vessels. Other methods of detection included having the lady in question drink milk from a woman who had borne a son. If she vomited, pregnancy was confirmed. Also grasping the lady's arm - if her veins were found to throb she was thought to be pregnant.

Ancient Greek and Roman Ladies of noble birth were encouraged to wear perfumed linen as underwear. If the lady's breath and nose smelt of the perfume the next morning, she was believed to be pregnant.

From the Middle Ages until the seventeenth century, aptly-named individuals known as 'Piss Prophets' claimed to diagnose pregnancy based on the colour and properties of urine. A 1552 European document described pregnancy urine as a *'clear pale lemon colour leaning toward off-white, having a cloud on its surface.'* A needle that turned black once it had been immersed in urine was another test, also sprinkling urine with sulphur – if worms suddenly appeared then the woman in question was thought to be pregnant. In yet another dubious test, a ribbon was dipped in the woman's urine and burned. If the smell nauseated her, a baby was on the way! Probably the most reliable 'Piss Prophet' test was mixing urine with white wine in order to observe its appearance - an off-white, cloudy mixture was thought to indicate pregnancy. Since wine does react with certain proteins, this was as close as anyone at the time came to getting it right.

In the 1890s, scientists were describing certain 'secretions'- later known as hormones - within the body which they felt were crucial to a woman's inner workings. Thirty years later it was observed, through scientific research into the sex hormones, that when the urine of pregnant women was injected into immature mice, rabbits, frogs and toads, it would create changes in the animals' ovaries. This is where the phrase 'The Rabbit Died' originated, as the rabbit or other small animal, would be killed and dissected to determine pregnancy. The presence of the pregnancy hormone hCG in a woman's urine induced ovulation in these animals. It is likely that a few small mammals died in order to ascertain if Princess Margaret was on her way in 1930. An improvement on 'The Rabbit Died' test arrived with the Frog Test in the 1930s. The urine of a potentially pregnant woman would be injected into a female frog. If the frog produced eggs within the next 24 hours, the woman was pregnant. Good news for the mother-to-be, also for the frog as it didn't die in the process. This was the only standard pregnancy test until the end of the 1950s so it's fair to say that it's thanks to a frog that the then Princess Elizabeth discovered she was pregnant with Prince Charles in 1948 – a Frog Prince, no less!

prince
Charles

By the 1960s when Princess Margaret's two children were born, a laboratory test that didn't involve animals but was very complicated, had been developed. Purified hCG (a hormone produced in pregnancy)was mixed with a urine sample along with antibodies directed against hCG. If a woman was pregnant, the red cells clumped together in a particular pattern.

In the 1970s – when Princess Anne was pregnant with Peter Phillips - a urine test was developed which displayed results in a few hours and which worked within days of a period being missed. This was the forerunner of the home pregnancy test which is now how most women - Royals and the rest - discover they are pregnant.

Did You Know?

There was a British Royal Baby Boom in 1963/4 with four members of the Windsor dynasty pregnant at the same time – Princess Alexandra gave birth to James Ogilvy on February 29 1964, The Queen had Prince Edward on March 10, the Duchess of Kent gave birth to Lady Helen Windsor (now Taylor) on April 28 and Princess Margaret delivered Lady Sarah Armstrong Jones (now Chatto) on May 1.

A Mixed Blessing

Not all Royal Ladies have been overjoyed to find themselves with child. Some, in fact, have been positively furious. . .

Eleanor of Acquitaine was not pleased to discover she was pregnant for a second time when she was married to her first husband, Louis of France. She didn't love him and had already tried to have the marriage annulled. However the Pope refused, preparing instead a special bed for Eleanor and Louis in which to sleep together. Baby girl Alix was born in the summer of 1151 but within nine months, the marriage was finally annulled and Eleanor married Henry II of England.

It wasn't so much pregnancy that *Marguérite Louise d'Orleans* Grand Duchess of Tuscany hated, it was her husband, Grand Duke Cosimo III. So desperate was Marguerite to end the marriage and return to her native France and also her lover, she unsuccessfully tried to induce a miscarriage while pregnant with daughter Anna Luisa Maria who was eventually born on August 11 1667. Then in 1671, while pregnant with her third child, Gian Gastone (later Duke of Tuscany), she tried to starve herself. But to no avail - Gian was born on May 24 1671. However when he was four, she left her husband and children, and finally returned to France.

Queen Victoria was livid when she discovered she was expecting her first child soon after her marriage to her beloved Albert .'*It is too dreadful,*' she wrote. '*I am really upset about it and it is spoiling my happiness as I have always hated the idea.*' Victoria went on to have eight more pregnancies in addition to this first one but she never enjoyed the experience. '*I think much more of our being like a cow or a dog at such moments,*' she wrote to her eldest daughter, Vicky. '*I positively think those ladies who are always "enceinte" quite disgusting; it is more like a rabbit or guinea-pig than anything else and really it is not very nice.*' Victoria herself was pregnant every other year for a total of 17 years!

Elisabeth, Empress of Austria and wife of Franz Joseph I, loved her children when they arrived but she abhorred being pregnant. According to a courtier, the Empress '*loathed the whole business.*' Obsessed with her own beauty, Elisabeth was so worried about pregnancy ruining her figure and making her ugly, she refused to be seen in public until well after the birth of her first child, Sophie, on March 5 1855.

Queen Mary, wife of George VI and the present Queen's grandmother, was not a fan of pregnancy although she succumbed to it six times. She described it as *'the penalty of being a woman'* and refused ever to discuss it.

Princess Anne, while (kind of) looking forward to the birth of her first child, Peter, in November 1977, she patently did not enjoy being pregnant. *'Being pregnant is a boring nine months,'* she said. *'I'm not particularly maternal. It's an occupational hazard of being a wife.'*

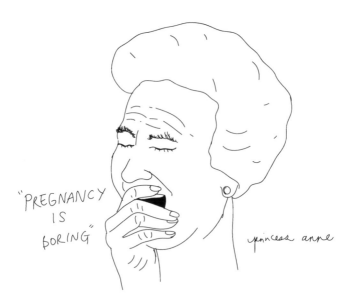

"PREGNANCY IS BORING"

princess anne

Did You Know?

Marie Antoinette loved being '*with child*'. In 1778 when five months pregnant she wrote, '*I am in excellent health and my child moved the first time on Friday July 31st at 10.30 at night: from that moment it has been moving often which causes me great joy.*'

—

CONSTANT CRAVINGS

It's not really known why pregnant women crave certain foodstuffs. The reasons may be hormonal, emotional, due to dietary deficiencies or a combination of all three. In the past – just as today - women-with-child were advised to steer clear of specific items for health reasons. Seventeenth century Queen Henrietta Maria, for instance, would have been instructed to cut down on her salt intake while pregnant as it was believed too much would cause her child to be born minus finger or toenails. Folkloric beliefs often regarded it as dangerous to deny a pregnant woman the kind of food she craved and family members would often go to great lengths to secure such cravings. Check out these Royal mum-to-be munchie requests. . .

Samphire. Edward IV's beautiful wife Elizabeth Woodville craved this asparagus-like, sea vegetable when pregnant with third daughter Cecily, born March 20 1469. A very healthy choice – samphire is rich in vitamins, especially vitamin C.

Apples. Anne Boleyn couldn't get enough apples when pregnant with daughter, the future Elizabeth I, born September 7 1533. In fact it was her passion for the pectin-heavy fruit that, she claimed, caused Henry VIII to suspect that his very new wife was pregnant. In Spring 1533 she announced that she had '*an inestimable wild desire to eat apples, such as she has never had in her life before*' and that King had told her it was a sign she was with child, but she had said it was nothing of the sort. Henry turned out to be right but Anne, being Anne, had probably just been teasing him all along.

Quail and Cucumber. Henry's third wife Jane Seymour liked to chow down on quail (a game bird) and cucumber when she was pregnant with the future Edward VI, born October 12 1537, although it's not known whether she liked to eat them together. Henry had crates of quail shipped in from Calais to satisfy his blossoming wife's cravings while her step daughter Mary brought Jane cucumbers from her own garden to crunch through.

Bacon Sandwiches. Diana's craving when pregnant with both William, born June 21 1982, and Harry, born September 15 1984. In a note to her chef, Mervyn Wycherley, she wrote *'To Mervie, please could I have a bacon sandwich for breakfast and a much-needed rest from our friend the tomato! D.'*

Cheeseburgers and Champagne, Mayonnaise Sandwiches, Mackerel Sandwiches. She may have been pregnant with Princess Beatrice, born August 8 1988, but Sarah Duchess of York, still fancied the fizz. Her gynaecologist was OK with this but suggested she limit her intake to three or four glasses per week rather than per evening! Her passion for sparkling wine was matched only by her desire for cheeseburgers – also sandwiches. *'When I was pregnant with my first* *daughter, Beatrice, I felt very large and important. I believed I had to eat for all of England! So my favourite thing to do to cure the doldrums was snack on my favourite treat, mayonnaise sandwiches, or my second-favourite treat, mackerel sandwiches. Yum!'* Towards the end of the pregnancy, Sarah had gained over 30 pounds in weight and struggled to squeeze into her size-16 (US 14) clothes. *'I looked like an elephant and felt fat and ugly,'* she said at the time.

Lavender Shortbread. Kate, Duchess of Cambridge, reportedly developed a sweet tooth during her pregnancy, and chowed down on lavender-enfused shortbread biscuits and chocolate.

Did You Know?

Princess Margaret gained 28 lbs in weight during each of her two pregnancies.

OF MORNING SICKNESS, MOOD SWINGS AND SWOLLEN ANKLES

Kate Cambridge may have had acute morning sickness but she's not the first Royal Lady to have suffered from the side-effects of pregnancy. . .

Queen Katherine Parr, sixth wife and widow of Henry VIII, was the (for then) grand old age of 36 when she became pregnant for the first time by fourth husband Thomas Seymour in 1547 – and she suffered. She was plagued by morning sickness and general discomfort throughout her pregnancy, necessitating her step-daughter Princess Elizabeth to write, '*what pain it is to you to write, your Grace being so great with child, and so sickly*'. Fourteen-year-old Elizabeth who, early on in Katherine's pregnancy, had been subject to Thomas Seymour's sexual advances, went on to wish Katherine '*a most lucky deliverance*'. It wasn't to be. While Katherine gave birth to a healthy baby girl, whom she named Mary, on August 30 1548, the former Queen died of childbed fever – the same condition that killed her sister-in-law, Queen Jane Seymour –

less than a week later. Little Mary Seymour is thought to have died in childhood.

Marie Antoinette enjoyed being pregnant and felt very well throughout her long-awaited first confinement, apart from the fact that, for a short while, she developed a kind of claustrophobia. '*I have an occasional feeling of stifling,*' she wrote to her mother when she was three months pregnant. She was reassured when she confided in her male midwife who told her she was allowed to take short carriage rides so long as they weren't too fast. However he insisted that she stay indoors on the days her period would have been due.

Queen Victoria was plagued by depression and volatile mood swings during her pregnancies. She complained of '*aches and sufferings. . . miseries and plagues,*' and felt '*so pinned down*' with her '*wings clipped*'. She would have terrible quarrels with her husband, Prince Albert, following him when he left the room in order '*to have it all out*'. He would then go to his room and proceed to write her a measured, reasonable letter, which would infuriate her even more. However when she'd calmed down, she would be filled with remorse. Although she hated being pregnant, she was upset when, after the birth of her ninth and final child, Princess Beatrice, on April 14 1857, her physician recommended that she have no more children. Victoria knew this would mean no more sex as Albert regarded it as a reproductive rather than recreational activity. '*Oh doctor,*' she reported to have said. '*Does this mean I can have no more fun in bed?*'

The Queen Mother, when Duchess of York, developed acrophobic tendencies while pregnant with Princess Margaret in 1930. '*My instinct is to hide in a corner when in this condition,*' she told her mother-in-law, Queen Mary, some months before Margaret was born on August 21 1930. '*I suppose it is a feeling handed down from many generations back. I should really like to live quietly in the country for the last few months and then reappear afterwards as if nothing had happened.*' Being a member of the Royal Family she was able to do just this.

Elizabeth
Duchess of York

Princess Diana suffered from morning sickness during both pregnancies. It was, however, much worse with Prince William as she was also bulimic at the time and, at just 20 years of age, having problems adjusting to her new life in addition to her condition. '*It was appalling,*' she said. '*Sick, sick, sick, sick, sick the whole time. Bulimia and morning sickness. Every time I stood up I was sick. I don't know what triggered it off. It was a very, very difficult pregnancy indeed and I felt the whole world was collapsing around me.*'

Sarah Ferguson, Duchess of York. During her pregnancy with Princess Beatrice in 1988, Fergie was diagnosed with high blood pressure and excessive water retention. A by-product of all those cheeseburgers and sandwiches, no doubt.

Did You Know?

———

When she started throwing up every morning shortly after her marriage to Crown Prince Ferdinand in 1893, 18-year-old Marie, the future Queen of Romania and a grand daughter of Queen Victoria, thought she was dying. She had no idea that she might be pregnant because no one had informed her how it happened.

FROM HERE TO MATERNITY

Kate's maternity wear has been very stylish but this certainly hasn't been the case with pregnant Royal Ladies throughout history. Until the thirteenth century, pregnant ladies of all classes – including Royal ones – wore their every-day clothes when with child. In those days, robes were made from flowing lengths of fabric and were seamless rather than cut and sewn to shape. As the belly began to billow, so did the cloth. But from the 1500s onwards, women's garments in the western world began to hug the figure more. A pregnant woman would let out her seams to allow for expansion. It was during the Baroque period from 1600-1750 that the first maternity dress was born. Known as the 'Adrienne' dress, it boasted fold after fold of voluminous fabric to accommodate a swelling baby belly. The fashion for high-waisted dresses during late Georgian and Regency eras was ideal for a pregnant Royal Lady such as Caroline of Brunswick, despised wife of George IV. During Victorian times, maternity clothes were designed to disguise the impropriety of pregnancy and special pregnancy corsets became popular. This trend of hiding one's pregnancy, particularly if a member of the Royal Family, continued until the 1970s with many a Princess, Queen and Duchess retiring from public view once they were visibly pregnant. Nevertheless there have still been some fascinating instances of how certain Royal Ladies have dressed, or rather disguised, their baby bumps.

Anne Boleyn was six months pregnant with the future Queen Elizabeth I when she was crowned Queen in a lavish four day ceremony in May/June 1533. But rather than disguising her pregnancy, Anne was one Royal Lady who wished to show off her bump. This baby – whom she and everyone else was convinced would be a boy - was proof that Henry VIII had been right to marry her. Her obvious fecundity was very much on show. Anne, whom Archbishop Cranmer noted '*is now somewhat big with child*', wore a gown of white cloth of gold for her ceremonial entry into London, which would surely have accentuated her pregnancy. It is said an extra panel of cloth had to be sewn into the gown to accommodate her growing figure.

Queen Mary, George V's Queen, was five months pregnant with her fourth child, Prince Henry, when her father-in-law, Edward VII, was crowned in Westminster Abbey in August 1902. Not that any one would have known. At the Coronation, her corset was as tightly laced as usual, therefore disguising and 'nipping-in' her baby bump. She surely can't have known that wearing tightly-laced, wasp-waisted corsets during pregnancy had been known to bring on miscarriage.

Pregnancy was still very much covered up in Royal circles in the 1950s. *Film star-turned-Princess of Monaco Grace Kelly* attempted to hide her swelling bump with her Hermes handbag when newly pregnant with Princess Caroline (born in January 1957). When the pregnancy was announced, a paparazzi shot of Grace – and the bag – made it onto the front of '*Life*' magazine, and the bag immediately became known as the '*Kelly bag*.'

Kelly hemes bag

Elizabeth II was still a Princess when pregnant with Prince Charles in 1948 and Princess Anne in

1950, and so able to hide away during pregnancy. That wasn't always possible once she was Queen and pregnant with Prince Andrew in 1959/60 and Prince Edward in '63/64 – although she did cancel the State Opening of Parliament on both occasions. Elizabeth was photographed in maternity wear in the 1960s but the cleverly designed two-piece suits and coats just made her looked bigger all over.

Princess Anne was the first major UK Royal to be 'out and proud' when expecting first baby, Peter, in 1977. No hiding herself away as her predecessors had done, the pregnant Anne carried on as normal and was, gasp, even photographed on official Royal business in the last few months of pregnancy – a large cream cape covering the bump. Ever practical and ever thrifty, Anne had Maureen Baker, designer of her 1973 wedding dress, alter her maternity wear so she could wear it once she was slim again. It was Anne who blazed the trail for the likes of Diana and Sarah Ferguson to be open about showing off their pregnancies.

Never mind 'Queen of Hearts', *Diana* was 'Queen of Smocks' when she was pregnant with Prince William in 1982 and took smock wearing to a whole new level. Polka-dot smocks, designer smocks, coat smocks, frilly smocks, plain smocks. . . The maternity smock market really swelled. By the time she was pregnant with Harry in 1984, Diana had become a little more sophisticated and her maternity-wear choices reflected this. However she couldn't resist wearing a few of her old favourites from time to time.

Sarah, Duchess of York did herself no favours in the wardrobe department when pregnant with Princess Beatrice in 1988. *'She looks like a tank!'* pronounced one fashion critic, and she was compared to a *'Chock-a-block Easter egg,'* by a female newspaper columnist who also advised the Duchess not to *'parade your pregnancy in a button-busting double breasted blazer and an almost bulge high mini skirt.'* Fergie has admitted that she ate for England, put on over 30 Ilbs and felt *'like an elephant'* during her first pregnancy but she didn't help herself by wearing normal clothes rather than maternity ones. She should have borrowed some of her sister-in-law's many smocks.

Did You Know?

Shortly before the birth of her first child in November 1840, Queen Victoria's shape was described by her obstetrician, Charles Locock, in less than complementary terms. *'Her figure is now most extraordinary. She goes without stays or anything that keeps her shape within bounds. She is more like a barrel than anything else.'*

Caution! Baby on Board

Certain Royal Ladies in the past have, for various reasons, taken unnecessary – sometimes foolhardy and even dangerous - risks during pregnancy. For most, it has been a matter of personal choice but for a few, their very lives – and that of their unborn babies – depended on it.

In March 1566 **Mary Queen of Scots** was six months pregnant with the future James I of England (VI of Scotland) when she rode pillion on horseback for five hours in the dead of night. She was fleeing for her life, following the murder of her secretary David Rizzio in her apartments at Holyrood House in Edinburgh. Although she'd no choice but to escape, Mary was

Mary Queen of Scots

one tough cookie. Her husband Lord Darnley had continually thrashed her horse and his own as they galloped, paying no heed to her pleadings. He callously told her that if she lost this child, they'd have others. When they finally arrived at Dunbar Castle – their destination – the first thing Mary did was order eggs for breakfast.

In late April 1644, the seven months pregnant **Queen Henrietta Maria**, wife of King Charles I, fled from Oxford where she and Charles had been living. England was in the grip of the Civil War and circumstance dictated that she part company with her husband at Abingdon – five-and-a-half miles west of Oxford. She was never to see him again. Henrietta Maria had intended to give birth to this, her ninth and last child, in Bath but was forced further west to Exeter as she feared being taken hostage by the Parliamentarians. After a difficult labour, during which it was not expected she would survive, the Queen gave birth to Princess Henrietta on June 26 1644.

Augusta, the 17-year-old wife of Frederick, Prince of Wales (eldest son of George II and Queen Caroline) was actually in labour when she and her husband fled from Hampton Court to St James' Palace in the early hours of August 31 1737. Fred, and therefore his young wife, was despised and hated by his parents who had kept the couple under virtual house arrest at Hampton Court. Caroline in particular was furious to discover they had absconded as she, doubting her son's ability to father a child, was determined to be present at the birth. But when she and her daughters arrived at St James', Augusta had already given birth to a daughter, also called Augusta. Caroline conceded the child must be Fred's as she was a *'poor little ugly she-mouse'* rather than a *'brave, large, fat, jolly boy'*.

In the Spring of 1819 when she was eight months pregnant, **Queen Victoria's mama, Victoire, Duchess of Kent,** made a mad dash across Europe in order that her child – possibly the future heir to the throne – would be born on British soil and therefore have his or her legitimacy declared by dignitaries. The strapped-for-cash Duke drove the 'Phaeton' coach himself in order to save money. In the coach behind them was Frau Siebold, a female obstetrician who had qualified as a surgeon – a rarity at the time. Fortunately the good Frau's expertise was not required en-route as the Duchess gave birth once she was safely at Kensington Palace, on May 24 1819.

Although she'd been advised to stay indoors and rest, seven months pregnant **Alexandra, Princess of Wales** was determined to watch her husband, Bertie, the future Edward VII, play ice hockey on the frozen Virginia Water in Surrey on January 8 1864. As Bertie played, Alix was whirled around the ice in a chair fitted with runners. Her pains started after luncheon and she wanted to go back to Frogmore House where they were staying, but Bertie pooh-poohed the idea and finished his game. By the time they returned to the house at 4pm, Alix was in labour proper. Five hours later, she delivered her first baby – a tiny 3lb little boy whom it was thought wouldn't survive. Against the odds, he did.

Sarah, Duchess of York. Gung-ho Fergie was five months pregnant with Princess Beatrice when she fell badly while skiing on a black run in Switzerland in March 1988. She landed on her back in a mountain stream but fortunately sustained no injuries although she was severely shaken. Then in July, a few weeks before Beatrice's birth, she was on her way to visit a friend when her Jaguar was rammed by a Ford Fiesta.

Diana, Princess of Wales, was three months pregnant with Prince William when she threw herself down the stairs at Sandringham House in early January 1982 after a massive row with husband, Prince Charles. She sustained severe bruising but the foetus was unharmed. Diana later said her behaviour had been '*a cry for help*'.

Did You Know?

Kate Middleton is a keen skier but unlike 'Aunty' Fergie, she decided against taking to the slopes when she was five months pregnant, and attending a society wedding in Switzerland. While the rest of the bridal party went on the 'piste', careful Kate took a gentle walk instead.

FAKING IT

Phantom pregnancy, false pregnancy, hysterical pregnancy, or to give it its medical name 'pseudocyesis', is a condition more common in dogs and mice than humans. But a number of Royal Ladies in history have been unfortunate enough to experience it, too. What causes it? There are various explanations, none of which is universally accepted because of the complex involvement of both physical and psychological factors. However doctors now suspect that it is the latter tricking the body into 'thinking' that it is pregnant. Certainly the following Royal Ladies were desperate to be pregnant when they believed themselves to be so.

Catherine of Aragon had been married to Henry VIII for only seven months when she miscarried a daughter on January 31 1510. The incident was not made public at the time and Catherine was convinced by her doctors that she was still pregnant - even when her periods resumed - and indeed her 'baby bump' continued to grow. Preparations for the birth began in earnest – the Royal nursery at Greenwich was refurbished and Catherine's apartments readied for her confinement. She '*took to her chamber*' some time in March 1510 – and waited and waited and waited. No baby arrived. Catherine's bump gradually disappeared and her confessor Fray Diego wrote, '*it has pleased our Lord to be her physician in such a way that the swelling decreased.*' Embarrassed and humiliated, Catherine remained in her chamber until the end of May. The final twist in this tale is that when she returned to court, she was actually approximately two months pregnant although she didn't know it at the time. She must have slept with Henry right up to the time she took to her chamber.

Anne Boleyn was under such pressure to produce a son, some believe she also had a false pregnancy. In April 1534 Lady Lisle wrote, '*The Queen hath a goodly belly, praying our Lord to send us a Prince*'. The pregnancy was again referred to in July 1934 then. . . nothing. There is no evidence of the outcome of this pregnancy apart from the fact that Imperial Ambassador, Eustace Chapuys, wrote at the end of September, '*Since the king began to doubt whether his lady was enceinte or not, he has renewed and increased the love he formerly had for a beautiful damsel of the court*'.

Mary I. Like mother, like daughter, Mary Tudor, offspring of Catherine of Aragon, also experienced a phantom pregnancy - but on two separate occasions.

A few months after her marriage to Philip of Spain in July 1554, a court doctor informed Mary that she was pregnant – her periods had stopped, her breasts were tender and supposedly producing milk, she felt sick, had gained weight and was convinced she felt 'the baby' move. She was ecstatic, although, at 38, she was concerned she would survive neither the pregnancy nor the birth. In April 1555, Mary went to Hampton Court for her confinement. On April 30, word got out that she'd given birth to a healthy son but when this was not confirmed, it became obvious it was not true. By May 21, Mary was still childless, still waiting in seclusion for the baby that never arrived. She wept that the Protestant heretics had bewitched her and that her child could not be born safely until they were all burned. It wasn't until August that Mary, her *'goodly belly'* now deflated, came out of confinement – and Philip left the country. She wasn't to see him again for two years. When he finally returned in 1557, it was only because he needed her support in his fight against France. Within a few months in autumn 1557, Mary, now 42, was writing to him to tell him she was pregnant. Not many believed her, including Philip, nevertheless for the next six months, there was a repeat of the events from 1555. By autumn '58, yet again any 'signs' of pregnancy had long disappeared and Mary was fading fast. She died of influenza at the end of the November. One train of thought is that Mary's 'pregnancies' were actually symptoms of ovarian or uterine cancer, or possibly the menopause, but this has never been proved.

In 1903 *Tsarina Alexandra of Russia,* desperate for a son after the birth of four daughters, believed herself to be pregnant again. There was talk of the baby arriving in August 1903 but no baby materialized. No conclusive reason was ever given for this – some sources suggested she'd had a miscarriage, others that she'd had a 'hysterical' or 'fantasy' pregnancy because she felt so much pressure to have a son. There were even rumours that she'd secretly given birth to a fifth daughter but had had the child adopted, believing that the Russian people would not accept yet another Grand Duchess.

Did You Know?

Anna Maria of Neuborg (1667-1740), second wife of the genetically challenged Spanish Charles II who was deformed due to family inbreeding, may not have had fake pregnancies but she regularly lied that she was having a child in order to dominate and extort money out of her husband.

III

ROYAL
BIRTHDAYS

———

*'I was as sick as a parrot
the whole way through labour'*

Diana, Princess of Wales on the birth of Prince
William, on 21 June 1982.

It takes a strong woman, whatever the hue of her blood, to keep it together during the heavy swell that is childbirth. Before the days of basic hygiene and sanitation, it was scarily life-threatening even if you were a Queen. The days when a delivery suite was a wood-panelled prison, when a labouring Royal Lady's waters were broken with the sharp edge of a coin or a midwife's grubby finger nail. When caesarean sections were only performed on dying women so that their unborn babies might survive, when a loss of blood always meant a loss of life and any kind of pain relief was regarded as sinful. Delicate Royal Ladies were thought to suffer more in childbirth than lower-born women. It was a class thing - the bluer your blood, the harder you had it. Until relatively recently there was additional pressure on labouring Royal Ladies. The fate of a Royal dynasty may well depend on the birth of a hale and hearty boy child. This was a Royal Wife's primary purpose in life, the reason they had been married to a Prince or King in the first place. There was evidence everywhere – in history and overseas - of dynasties that had died out because no heir had been produced. Under such pressure it wasn't always easy for a Queen to keep her head. Today's Royal mothers and mothers-to-be don't know they're born. . .

Did You Know?

The Queens of Ancient Egypt gave birth balancing on two large bricks between which a vessel of boiling water would be placed. The steaming vapours were thought to hasten labour and ease the pain but, eeeew, just imagine the scalding!

—

CONFINEMENT SPACES

Throughout history Royal Ladies have had special spaces in which to give birth. The Queens of Ancient Egypt retreated into 'birthing' bowers when they went into labour. Such rooms would be decorated with images of Hathor, the goddess of fertility and childbirth, and Bes, god of the household. Religion continued to be a very real presence in the birthing chamber – for Royalty at least. From medieval times to the seventeenth century, a Royal mother-to-be would withdraw into her 'lying-in' chamber approximately six-to-four weeks before she was due to give birth. She would not emerge until her 'churching' ceremony, at which she would be 'cleansed' of childbirth, a month after the birth. Once inside the chamber, shutters and windows would be closed, key holes stopped up, and tapestries hung to ensure the room was airtight, therefore making it impossible for evil spirits to enter. By the eighteenth century, the dark lying-in chamber had largely been abandoned in favour of a bright, airy birthing room in order to minimise infection and disease. A Royal Lady's bed chamber was generally the delivery room of choice and remained so until the last quarter of the 20th century when Royal babies started to be born in hospital – their mothers following the trend for once rather than setting it. But not all Royal Ladies in history have laboured by the rules.

The Tent. Constance, a twelfth century Queen of Sicily and Germany, gave birth to her only child, the future Holy Roman Emperor Frederick II, in a specially-erected tent in the market square of the Italian town of Jesi on December 26 1194. Over 40-years-old at the time of her confinement and nick-named 'The Barren Queen', she knew many would doubt the child was really hers. So she had a semi-public birth and invited the town's matrons to witness it.

The Building Site. Caernarfon Castle in Wales was a new-build-in-progress when Eleanor of Castile,

Constance and her
birthing tent

the first wife of Edward I, gave birth to their 14th
child, the future Edward II, there on April 25 1284.
As a result, the Queen's lying-in chamber was little
more than a windowless den measuring 12' x 8', built
within the thickness of the castle's walls. Eleanor had
tapestries hung from the walls to cheer the room up
and, in doing so, set a trend. She was the first person
in England to use tapestries as wall hangings.

The Cellar. Elizabeth Woodville, consort of Yorkist
King Edward IV, had planned to give birth to their
fourth child in the sumptuous Palace of Westminster.
But when the Lancastrian Henry VI was restored to

the throne in autumn 1470, forcing Edward into exile, a heavily pregnant Elizabeth, her mother Jacquetta and three little daughters sought sanctuary in a *'dismal'* basement-like dwelling in the grounds of Westminster Abbey. It was here she gave birth to the future Edward V on November 2 1470.

The Private House. Born April 21 1926, Elizabeth II is the first British monarch ever to have been born in a private house rather than Royal castle or palace. With building works ongoing at the Grosvenor Square mansion rented by her parents, the future George VI and Queen Elizabeth (then Duke and Duchess of York), the mother-to-be preferred to give birth at the Mayfair home of her parents, 17 Bruton Street, rather than labour at the Royal in-laws palace.

The Kitchen Table. On June 10 1921, Philippos, Prince of Greece and Denmark, fifth child and only son of Prince and Princess Andrew of Greece, and the future Duke of Edinburgh, was born a-top the kitchen table in 'Mon Repos', a rundown rented summer villa situated on the Greek island of Corfu. The house had no electricity, hot water or indoor plumbing, and the family were so short of cash they had trouble paying the rent. A year later, they left the dilapidated pile with Philip travelling in a carry cot made from an old orange box.

The Mocked-up Hospital Ward. The Belgian Suite in Buckingham Palace was transformed into a temporary hospital ward for the birth of Prince Charles on November 14 1948 – and was again for the births of Prince Andrew on February 19 1960 and Prince Edward on March 10 1964.

The Library. On January 23 1957, Princess Grace gave birth to daughter Caroline in the library of the Princes' Palace in Monaco, which had been turned into a makeshift delivery suite for the occasion.

Did You Know?

On July 5 1321 Isabella of France, the Queen of England's Edward II, gave birth to her fourth child and second daughter, Joan, in the rain. She had chosen to 'be confined' at the Tower of London which at the time was run down and dilapidated. Rain poured through the roof of the Queen's apartments and into the Royal birthing chamber, soaking Isabella as she laboured.

BIRTHING PARTNERS

Until the middle of the seventeenth century, childbirth was a strictly 'Women Only' affair for Royal Ladies – and every other mother-to-be for that matter. Midwives rather than physicians would deliver the Regal offspring and these women, who had learned their trade by assisting at births since childhood rather than studying textbooks, would often attend Royal Birth after Royal Birth. A Royal mother-to-be would have also been accompanied by many other birthing partners - ladies-in-waiting, wet-nurses and nurses-in-waiting, dry-nurses, rockers of the Royal cradle, laundresses, female family members and friends. This gang of women were known as 'God's Sibs' as in God's Siblings which, over time, became abbreviated to 'Gossips'. Change came about in the seventeenth century with the invention of obstetric instruments such as forceps, and also the arrival of male doctors, who had started to formally study the business of childbirth. These men began to nudge midwives into a supporting role as science started to be revered above the natural process that was birth. Royal Ladies embraced this change enthusiastically but the presence of men, even if they were doctors, affected the way they gave birth. By the time Victoria was on the throne in the 1840s, most respectable middle and upper class women laboured and delivered their babies facing away from their physician, as Victoria herself did, in order to preserve their modesty. Happily those days are long gone and in the twenty first century, Royal, and non-Royal, mothers-to-be have complete control over who is with them when they give birth. It was not always so. . .

Elizabeth Woodville. Giving birth to her son Prince Edward (born November 2 1470) in a cramped cellar meant that the Edward IV's Queen was unable to have the numerous ladies, midwives, baby nurses and wet-nurses-in-waiting she would normally have called on as birthing partners. In the event, just her faithful attendant, Lady Scrope and, Mother Cobb, a midwife, were with her.

Henrietta Maria. The first labour of Charles I's Queen in May 1629 did not go to plan as her accomplished midwife, Madame Perrone, failed to arrive from Henrietta's native France in time. A local midwife was summoned but collapsed under the strain! Although Henrietta Maria's labour was rapid, the baby boy she bore died a few hours after his birth on May 13, and it took the Queen weeks to recover. As a result Henrietta ensured Madame Perrone was always safely in the country when she was due to give birth.

Queen Mary Beatrice. While it was law for court officials to be present at a Royal birth in order to witness the legitimacy of the child, said officials generally waited in a room adjoining the delivery chamber. Not so with poor Mary Beatrice, consort to James II, when she gave birth to Prince James Francis Edward on June 10 1688 . Suspicious of James and Mary's Catholicism and in light of a rumour circulating around court that the Queen was faking her pregnancy, a total of 67 people – including lords, ladies and a dowager Queen in addition to the obligatory midwives and baby nurses - took up pole positions in Mary's Beatrice bedroom at St James' Palace as she went into labour.

Marie Antoinette. When France's most famous Queen gave birth to her first child, Marie Therese Charlotte, on December 18 1778, most of the court was present to witness it. As soon as doctors announced the Queen was about to give birth, there was a stampede which guards were unable to control. According to Marie Antoinette's attendant, '*The persons who poured into the chamber were so numerous that the rush nearly killed the Queen. It was impossible to move about the* *chamber, which was filled with so motley a crowd that one might have fancied himself in some place of public amusement. Two chimney-sweeps climbed upon the furniture for a better sight of the Queen'.* As a result, Marie Antoinette passed out and leeches were applied to her body in order to bleed her.

Princess Alice was the third child of Queen Victoria and Prince Albert, and the great grandmother of the Duke of Edinburgh. At Windsor Castle on April 6 1863, Alice gave birth to her first child, named Victoria after her grandmother, who, along with Alice's husband

Prince Louis of Hesse, had witnessed the birth. For the Queen, it was a case of déjà vu as Alice gave birth in the same bed and room in which she herself had laboured, and Alice also wore the same night shift Victoria had worn for each of her nine confinements. '*It seemed a strange dream and as if it must be me and dearest Papa – instead of Alice and Louis,*' wrote Victoria. The Queen was an enthusiastic doula or birth attendant. Wherever possible she insisted on being present when a daughter or daughter-in-law gave birth.

Princess Alexandra, the wife of the future Edward VII, gave birth to their first child, Prince Albert Victor, two months prematurely on January 8 1864 at Frogmore House near Windsor. So unexpected was the birth, Alexandra's lady-in-waiting, Lady Macclesfield, was forced to send for the local doctor as the six doctors who had been booked to deliver the baby two months hence were obviously not in attendance. As it turned out, the local doctor didn't arrive in time and, just before 9pm, Lady Mac, as she was known, delivered the tiny baby onto her own red flannel petticoat which she'd removed for the purpose. While Prince Albert Victor (known in the family as Eddy) and her first daughter, Louise, genuinely were premature, it is thought Alexandra pretended her other children were, too, in order to stop her interfering mother-in-law, Queen Victoria, from being present at their births!

Elizabeth II. Midwife Helen Rowe, or 'Rowie' as the Queen fondly called her, was present at all four of Her Majesty's labours. The Queen wrote how '*pleased and relieved*' she was that Rowie was always able to be in attendance.

Did You Know?

In 1948, before the birth of his first grandchild, Prince Charles, King George VI was persuaded by his private secretary, 'Tommy' Lascelles, to dispense with the 340-year-old tradition of the Home Secretary and other officials being in attendance – or at least waiting in a nearby room – in order to witness and verify every Royal birth. His wife Elizabeth was not happy, writing to Lascelles, - '*We should cling to our domestic traditions and ceremonies for dear life.*' She was finally persuaded when Lascelles wrote back that the presence of officials at such an intimate time was '*an unwarrantable and out of date intrusion into Your Majesties private lives*'.

OF BREECH BIRTHS AND
CAESAREAN SECTIONS

A breech birth is a bottom or feet first delivery - literally an 'upside down' birth. Historically, 'a breech' or malpresentation was regarded with alarm – even in Royal households. Midwives and medics would attempt to 'turn' the baby manually, as indeed they often do today, but then, unlike now, the practise was a danger in itself. For years it was thought the position of the unborn child would right itself if the labouring mother was rolled around on her bed, shaken vigorously or repeatedly tossed into the air from a blanket – 13-year-old Margaret Beaufort was subjected to this last practise as she laboured with the future Henry VII in January 1457. Breech babies were also rotated in the birth canal – an agonising process endured by Vicky, Princess Victoria, the eldest child of Victoria and Albert, when she was giving birth to her first child, the future Kaiser Wilhelm II in January 1859. Not surprisingly, her wails and screams could be heard echoing around the Kronprinzenpalais in Berlin and the baby finally emerged with a damaged left arm. Wilhelm survived the ordeal of his birth, as did Richard III, another breech baby born on October 2 1452 but others, such as Prince Charles James, the

wahhh Wahhh Wahhl Wahhl Wahh Wahh

kronze prinzepalaia

first child of Charles I and Henrietta Maria, did not.
He died within hours of his birth on May 13 1629.
By the early twentieth century, medical advances
meant that the caesarean section, a surgical procedure
in which one or more incisions are made through
a mother's abdomen and uterus wall, became a
successful way to deliver a breech baby. The caesarean
or c-section originated in Ancient Rome where the law
required that the child of a mother who had died in
childbirth should be cut from her womb. It evolved
into a way of saving an unborn child. Contrary to
popular belief, Roman Dictator Julius Caesar was not
born by a c-section as his mother would never have
survived - and indeed she did. Caesarean deliveries
for breech babies and other complicated pregnancies

started going mainstream after the Queen Mother, the Duchess of York, gave birth to the future Elizabeth II, a breech baby, by c-section on April 21 1926. But little Lilibet was not the only one. . .

Robert II of Scotland. The first British Royal to be born by caesarean - and the last for over 600 years, Robert was delivered at Paisley Abbey on March 2 1316 when his 19-year-old mother, Marjorie Bruce, was either dying, or already dead, following a fall from a horse. A myth grew up that Jane Seymour gave birth by c-section to the future Edward VI on October 12 1537. Not so. Jane would never have survived the birth. She died of puerperal fever when Edward was 12-days -old.

Elizabeth II. A breech baby with whom her mother, the then Duchess of York, laboured for many hours before doctors deemed that that 'certain line of treatment' was necessary in the early hours of April 21 1926. The Duchess also opted for the same 'line of treatment' when she gave birth to Princess Margaret on August 21 1930.

Prince Charles. The fountains in Trafalgar Square ran blue after the birth of Prince Charles on November

14 1948 but the little Prince had reportedly given his mother a hard time – a long, drawn-out labour followed by a c-section delivery. Like his mother, he Charles is thought to have been a breech presentation. The Queen's subsequent three children – Anne (August 15 1950), Andrew (February 19 1960) and Edward (March 10 1964) – were also born by caesarean.

David Viscount Linley & *Lady Sarah Chatto*. It wasn't for medical reasons that Princess Margaret had c-sections when she gave birth to both David (born November 3 1961) and Sarah (born May 1 1964). Image-conscious Margaret did not approve of natural childbirth because it meant the babies wouldn't arrive in the world looking perfect!

Princess Eugenie. A 'breecher' like granny the Queen, her mother Sarah's gynaecologist at the Portland Hospital in London was unable to turn her and she was born by caesarean on March 23 1990.

Lady Louise Mountbatten Windsor. Lady Louise was born a month prematurely on November 8 2003 and delivered by emergency caesarean. Her mother, the Countess of Wessex, had been rushed by ambulance to Frimley Park hospital in Surry when her placenta broke up in-utero, causing severe blood loss to mother and daughter. Louise's younger brother, James Viscount Severn, was also born by c-section at the same hospital on December 17 2007.

Did You Know?

A medieval German Empress heard that whipping brought on labour but unwilling to be whipped herself, she subjected 20 men servants to the ordeal. Two of them died in the process but at least she went into labour!

No Pain No Gain

Until approximately 150 years ago, it was believed that all mothers-to-be, Royal ones included, deserved to suffer in childbirth. As was stated in the book of Genesis 3:16: *'To the woman he said, "I will greatly increase your pains in childbearing; with pain you will give birth to children".'* Labour pains were, it was thought, God's way of punishing for Eve taking a bite of that apple and thus causing all mankind to suffer. It was the unlikely Royal figure of Queen Victoria who helped put a stop to this misogynistic madness by embracing chloroform as pain relief when she had her eighth child, Prince Leopold, in April 1853. Since then, of course, the range and effectiveness of methods of pain relief in labour have improved beyond measure. Gas and air, pethidine, epidural anaesthesia - every mother-to-be, can, if she so wishes, experience a virtually pain-free birth. State-of-the-art homeopathy and hypnosis techniques may also be of use. Before Victoria, however, labouring Royal Ladies – and therefore every other woman in childbirth – had only a combination of folk remedies, herbal draughts, symbolism, spells, potions and talismans to fall back on. That and blind faith. . .

Amulets. The labouring Queens of Ancient Egypt wore talismans representing their sacred deities. Amulets were practically the only thing these Egyptian 'mummies' did wear while giving birth. Fragments of painted plaster from a birth house show a Queen of the Nile cradling her newborn, naked apart from a collar around her neck and a girdle around her hips. Spells for protection during childbirth have also been found on fragments of papyrus, for example – *'Come down, placenta, come down! I am Horus who conjures in order that she who is giving birth becomes better than she was, as if she was already delivered!'* This was to be repeated four times over a dwarf made of clay, known as the *'Bes-amulet'*, which was placed on the brow of the woman in labour.

Potions. Roman Empresses looked to gory, animal-inspired potions to help ease their labour pangs. According to Pliny the Elder, a Roman philosopher and naturalist, fat from hyena loins produced an immediate delivery for a woman in difficult

Sneezing was thought to ease labour pains in Roman times

labour. Also recommended was a drink sprinkled with powdered sow's dung, another made from goose semen or alternatively she could imbibe *'the liquids that flow from a weasel's uterus through its genitals'*. Sneezing was also thought to help! This childbirth 'quackery' continued well into the seventeenth century with some midwives and physicians even recommending that a labouring woman *'take a good draught of her husband's urine'* in order to procure a speedy, hopefully painfree birth.

Birth Girdles. Big in the Middle Ages, these belts were religious relics thought to have been worn by the mothers of various saints and holy figures. It was believed that donning such a pious piece of cloth would surely ease labour pains! Parish churches hired out whatever birth girdles they happened to have in their possession but England's Queens had access to the truly 'top-notch' ones. The 'Our Lady Girdle', donated to Westminster Abbey by Edward the Confessor in the eleventh century and believed to have been worn by the Virgin Mary herself, was dispatched to Gascony when Eleanor of Provence, Henry III's Queen, gave birth to her daughter, Beatrice, on June 24 1242. It was worn again in 1303 by Edward I's youngest daughter, Elizabeth, for the birth of her son, Hugh. And as she laboured with the future Henry VIII in late June 1491, Elizabeth of York paid the Benedictine monks of the Abbey 16 shillings (the equivalent of £3500 today) for its hire.

Prayer. Medieval Queens were encouraged to call upon the saints for help during childbirth. Thomas of Brotherton, born June 1 1300, the son of Edward I and Marguerite of France, was named after St. Thomas Becket, whose name his mother had cried out during labour and whom she credited with easing her pains. St Margaret, the patron saint of childbirth, was also regularly called upon, and several Princesses including Margaret, the future Queen of Scotland (born 1240), Margaret Tudor (Henry VIII's elder sister born 28 November 1489), and Margaret, ninth child and sixth daughter of Edward I (born September 11 1327) were named for her. In January 1245, the fourth child of Henry III and Eleanor of Provence was named Edmund, after St Edmund whose name was continually chanted throughout her labour.

Symbolism. Not pain relief as such but the attendants of medieval Royal Ladies would try and help things along by opening cupboards and drawers, unlocking doors and chests, and untying knots - acts which were, they believed, symbolic of opening the womb. Crystals, precious and semi-precious stones and metals were also clutched at in the hope they would offer some respite. Some hope!

Magic. It wasn't unheard of for Royal Ladies, or rather their attendants, to meddle with magic in order to try and alleviate labour pains. As Mary Queen of Scots gave birth to her only child, James, in June 1566, her attendant, the Countess of Atholl, attempted to cast the pangs of childbirth onto a certain Lady Reres who was also in the throes of labour at the Scottish court. Lady Reres' pains increased - but then so did the Queen Mary's! Ironically baby James, when King James VI of Scotland, became a virulent opponent of the use of spells in childbirth. In 1590 one of his subjects, an Edinburgh gentlewoman named Eufame MacAlyane, was suffering unbearable pain during the birth of her twin sons. In desperation, she sought relief from Agnes Sampson, a midwife with 'healing properties' but whom James was convinced was a witch. When he was informed of Agnes's involvement in Eufame's labour, the King ordered the execution of both women. They were burned alive on Castle Hill, Edinburgh in January 1591.

Chloroform. Queen Victoria was hardly a trailblazer for women's emancipation but she broke one birth taboo single-handedly. For the birth of her eighth child, Prince Leopold in April 1853, she employed the services of Dr John Snow, a Yorkshire farmer's son, who had pioneered the use of chloroform as an anaesthetic. Her obstetrician, Sir Charles Locock, had grave doubts, not least because of Dr Snow's humble origins, but Victoria overruled him. She found '*oh that blessed chloroform. . .soothing and delightful beyond measure*' and insisted Dr Snow again be in attendance when she gave birth to Princess Beatrice four years later. Victoria's decision was not universally approved. Protests were staged on religious and medical grounds but the procedure gained popularity and became known as the 'Anaesthesia de la Reine'. Victoria advised all her female descendents to give birth under the influence of the '*soothing*' and '*delightful*' drug.

Twilight Sleep. This mix of morphine and scopolamine was widely used in childbirth from 1905 onwards. It didn't kill the pain of labour but the mother-to-be would have had no memory of it. It was reported the Queen Mother was 'twilighted' as she laboured with Princess Margaret in August 1930 but this was strenuously denied. The private secretary of the then Duke and Duchess of York wrote to the press to protest that such stories were *'absolutely without any foundation and have caused Their Royal Highnesses the greatest possible annoyance.'*

Epidural. Oh, that blessed epidural! Certainly contemporary Royal Ladies have had no qualms about having a spinal injection of anaesthesia to numb the pain of childbirth. Princess Diana embraced it when her temperature soared while giving birth to Prince William. Ditto her sister-in-law Sarah Duchess of York when she gave birth to Beatrice on August 8 1988, *'My labour was not simple or easy. Beatrice went into a stressed situation halfway down the birth canal and we were 60 seconds away from a caesarean. Thankfully she continued on happily to a normal birth, though I had an epidural,'* Sarah later recalled.

Did You Know?

Princess Alexandra, wife of the future Edward VII, was not allowed *'soothing, delightful'* chloroform as she laboured with her third child, Princess Louise, in February 1867. Seriously ill with rheumatic fever and suffering from intense pain in her hips and legs - in addition to labour pain - her doctors felt administering the drug would be dangerous in light of her weakened condition.

THE LONG AND THE SHORT OF IT

Although a trickily-positioned baby may slow down the birth process, there has never been any medical explanation as to why some labours are shockingly quick while others are interminably slow. Modern medical practise in the form of induction may help speed up labour but intervention isn't new. A medieval midwife rubbed her Royal Lady's belly with oils and unguents in order to hasten birth, or she deftly used her stiletto-like, specially-grown fingernail to break the waters. She would have urged her Lady to go up and down stairs for an hour; massaged, stretched and dilated the genital area and birth canal; and, once her patient was sitting on the birthing stool, pressed on the belly to push the child downwards. Birth was usually expected within 20 contractions or 'pangs'. If it took longer, the drawer-opening and knot-untying routine would start.

While some Regal mothers-in-waiting have given birth in less time than it took to dress their hair, for others the time really did drag. . .

the medieval mid-wife's tool of her trade

Ninety Minutes. On November 8 1768, Queen Charlotte, consort to George III, gave birth to Princess Augusta Sophia, in just an hour-and-a-half. But then the Princess was her seventh child.

Two Hours. The labour time of James II's second wife, Queen Mary Beatrice, when she gave birth to James Francis Edward, Prince of Wales (The Old Pretender) on June 10 1688.

Three Hours. On May 13 1629 Queen Henrietta Maria, consort to Charles I, pushed out her first baby in just three hours. It did, however, take her the same number of weeks for her to recover and the baby died within hours of his birth.

Six Hours. A popular length of labour with Royal Ladies. Princess Grace of Monaco with Princess Caroline (January 23 1957), the Queen Mother with Princess Margaret (August 21 1930), Victoire, Duchess of Kent with the future Queen Victoria (May 19 1819).

Nine Hours. The duration of Anne Boleyn's labour with the future Queen Elizabeth I on September 7 1533, also the length of Princess Diana's labour with Harry on September 15 1984.

Twelve Hours. The time taken by Caroline of Brunswick, the Prince Regent's despised wife, to give birth to Princess Charlotte on January 7 1796. Also the length of Queen Victoria's labour on giving birth to her first child, Princess Victoria 'Vicky', on November 21 1840.

Fourteen Hours. Marie Louise of Austria had a tough time giving birth to the future King of Rome on March 20 1811. Although weak at birth, the infant King was, by all accounts, a good size.

Fifteen Hours. Princess Victoria, the Crown Princess of Prussia, and Victoria and Albert's eldest child, almost died giving birth to her first child Wilhelm, the future Kaiser Wilhelm II, on January 27 1859, despite the administrations of the British doctors and midwives especially despatched from Britain by Queen Victoria.

Sixteen Hours. Diana's *sick as a parrot* labour when she gave birth to Prince William on June 21 1982.

Twenty Four Hours. Queen Elizabeth, the Queen Mother, went into labour on the evening of April 20 1926 but it would be another, very long and painful day before her doctors decided to perform a Caesarean, in order to deliver the breech baby destined to be Elizabeth II on April 21.

Thirty Hours. The duration of Queen Elizabeth II's labour with Prince Charles in November 1948. Finally, like-mother-like-daughter, a *'certain procedure'* was carried out.

Three Days. A seemingly endless labour for Jane Seymour when she gave birth to the future Edward VI in October 1537. A large procession took place in London during this time to pray for the Queen's deliverance from a difficult labour.

Did You Know?

After the birth of Albert and Victoria's ninth child, Beatrice, in April 1857, Albert was warned by her medic, Dr Clark, that he feared for Victoria's sanity if she had another baby. Albert duly took note – Beatrice was their last child.

ABSENT FATHERS

Until the 1970s, it was rare for any father-to-be to witness his child being born. However some Royal fathers-to-be, being all-powerful, have, throughout history, made their own rules, choosing to venture into the birthing chamber years and sometimes centuries before it became common practise. James II, the Duke of Kent - father of Victoria, Prince Albert, Prince George - father of the current Duke of Kent, and Prince Louis of Hesse were all present at some or all of their children's births. Prince Albert was, according to Victoria, the perfect Doula. '*There could be no kinder, wiser nor more judicious nurse,*' she wrote after their first child was born in November 1840. The majority of Royal Sires, however, whether through preference or protocol, steered well clear until it became standard practise for dads to be there. By the dawn of the twenty first century, 95% of fathers in the western world were in attendance at their babies' births. Captain Mark Phillips, Princess Anne's first husband, was the first father-to-be in recent years to be present at a Royal birth when son Peter, the Queen's first grandchild, was born on November 15 1977. The experience, he commented afterwards, was '*not everyone's cup of tea*'. Maybe not but since then almost every expectant Royal father has witnessed his child coming into the world – an exception being Prince Edward, Earl of Wessex, who was out of the UK in November 2003 when his wife Sophie unexpectedly went into labour a month early with Lady Louise. For Prince Charles, witnessing the birth of Prince William in June 1982 was an unforgettable experience, and he said shortly afterwards, '*I'm so honoured I was beside Diana's bedside the whole time because I really felt I shared deeply in the process of birth and as a result was rewarded by seeing a small creature that belonged to us even though he seemed to belong to everyone else, too.*' It was very different for some Kings and Princes...

Henry II. He was keeping Christmas in France when his wife, Eleanor of Aquitaine, gave birth to their eighth and final child, John, on Christmas Eve 1166 in Oxford, and, given the circumstances, you can't help but wondering if he'd run off in order to save himself a tongue-lashing. Eleanor had planned to give birth at Woodstock Palace in Oxfordshire but swiftly made alternative arrangements when she discovered Henry had allowed his mistress, the '*fair*' Rosamund de Clifford, to live there.

Henry VIII. Given how desperate he was for a son,

one should have thought Henry would have been in the same Palace (Hampton Court) as his third wife, Jane Seymour, when she went into labour in October 1537. He was, instead, at the Esher residence of his chief minister, Thomas Cromwell, only arriving at Hampton Court once he knew the child was a boy. If the baby had been yet another girl, odds are he wouldn't have bothered.

James V of Scotland. While his wife, Mary of Guise, was in the throes of a premature labour with the future Mary Queen of Scots at Linlithgow Castle in early December 1552, James was 40 miles away at Falkland Palace, in the throes of a nervous breakdown. He had just suffered a crushing defeat by his auld enemy, the English, but was also prone to hysteria. He never saw his daughter. Six days after his wife had given birth, 30-year-old James was dead.

Napoleon. During the long labour of second wife, Marie-Louise, as she tried to give birth to the future King of Rome in March 1011, the stressed-out, pocket-sized Emperor of France allowed himself the luxury of a long, hot soak in the bath tub. Famously he preferred his wives not to bathe. '*Don't wash,*' he wrote to first wife Josephine when returning from battle. '*I'm coming home.*'

George V. In June 1894 while his '*darling May*' (later Queen Mary) was pushing out the future Duke of Windsor in a bedroom at White Lodge, Richmond Park, the then Duke of York was pretending to read '*Pilgrim's Progress*' in the library.

Duke of York
1894

pilgrims
progress

Prince Philip. While his wife, the then Princess Elizabeth, laboured with the soon-to-be Prince Charles on November 14 1948, the Duke of Edinburgh was smashing his way around a Squash court. He was holed-up in his Buckingham Palace study when Prince Andrew was born on February 19 1960 – the Queen allegedly wanted her husband well out of the way.

Did You Know?

Following the birth of his first daughter and fourth child in autumn 1766, George III was so desperate to have a second baby girl he insisted on interrupting his wife's labour in November 1768 in order to '*demand*' another daughter of her doctors. Happily for all concerned, the baby did turn out to be female.

After Birth

Much rejoicing has traditionally followed the birth of a Royal baby, providing both mother and child are healthy, that is. Beyond the Palace or hospital walls, the gun salutes fire off their rounds of celebratory ammunition, crowds gather and the world delights in wetting the baby's head. When Henry VIII's longed-for male heir was finally born on October 12 1537, for instance, free wine flowed on the streets of London. Within the inner sanctums of the Royal birthing chamber or delivery room, the post-natal scenes have usually been equally joyous – on November 14 1948 George VI was so delighted his darling daughter Lilibet had given birth to son and heir, Prince Charles, the King could be heard cheering loudly as he entered the Buckingham Palace suite which had been turned into a temporary hospital ward for the event. However for some Royal Families, post-natal joy has sadly been very much confined. . .

Henry VI. Henry's father, King Henry V, should have been ecstatic when news reached him in France that his wife, Katherine de Valois, had given birth in England to a healthy son on December 6 1421. Indeed he was until he found out exactly where his son had been born – Windsor Castle. On leaving for France six months earlier, Henry the elder had given his wife strict instructions to be confined at any Castle or Palace but Windsor. He had, it seemed, studied the planets and deemed that destiny would not favour a child born at Windsor around the time Katherine was due to give birth. The King is said to have sighed deeply and recited the following verse to his Chamberlain: '*I, Henry, born at Monmouth, shall small time reign, and much get; But Henry of Windsor shall long reign, and lose all of it.*' His words turned out to be eerily prophetic. Henry V reigned for just nine years but was victorious at the Battle of Agincourt, gaining the French throne for England, and he was also immortalised by Shakespeare. Henry VI, his unfortunate son, however, although King for a total of 20 years, succumbed to madness, lost everything his father had gained and, in 1471, was murdered in the Tower of London.

Edward, Prince of Wales. While the birth of Henry VI's own son on October 13 1453 was celebrated by the nation, it brought no joy to the King himself. The month before, Henry had suffered a mental breakdown that lasted for more than a year and he failed to respond to his son and heir. Edward became known as '*the child of sorrow and infelicity.*'

James Francis Edward, Prince of Wales. After the Catholic Prince was born in St James' Palace on June 10 1688, a rumour rapidly spread that a warming pan, brought into the chamber before his mother Queen Mary Beatrice had delivered, was the vehicle by which a changeling child had been smuggled into the palace - the inference being that Mary Beatrice had given birth to a stillborn child or never been pregnant at all. The baby Prince's half-sister, the protestant Princess Anne, who hadn't even been present at the birth, was chief rumour-monger. Mary Beatrice, a Catholic like her husband James II, was upset and confused by her stepdaughter's malicious talk. There was no truth in the rumour but Anne and her sister Mary swore that there was in order to win the crown away from their father and his son. They succeeded. Within six months, the abdicating King, his wife and baby son had fled to France.

Mary Beatrice's changeling child?

Grand Duke Paul of Russia. In September 1754, after a difficult labour, the future Catherine the Great finally gave birth to an heir, Paul. Within minutes the Empress Elizabeth, the baby's great aunt, snatched him up and took him to another part of the Winter Palace in St Petersburg. Catherine was left alone, lying in bloody sheets without so much as a glass of water. She wasn't allowed to see her baby or even ask about his welfare as this would have implied she didn't trust the Empress.

Dauphin Louis Joseph. Louis XVI was overjoyed when Marie Antoinette finally presented him with a son and heir on October 22 1781 but for the Queen, it was bitter-sweet. After cradling him in her arms for the first time, she handed the baby to an attendant, saying, *'Take him for he belongs not to me but to the country'*.

Princess Charlotte of Wales. Three days after her birth on January 7 1796, her father, the future George IV, changed his will, entrusting the care of his newborn daughter to his parents and decreeing that his wife *'should in no way either be concerned in the education or care of the child.'* He also bequeathed all his wife's jewels to their daughter and announced that '*I had rather see toads and vipers crawling over my victuals than sit at the same table as her (Caroline).*'

Prince Harry. According to Princess Diana, Prince Charles wasn't exactly bowled over by the arrival of his second-born son on September 15 1984. '*Charles always wanted a girl but I knew Harry was a boy because I saw it on the scan,*' she said. '*His first comment was, "Oh God, it's a boy", second comment "and he's even got red hair". Something inside me closed off.*' Prince Charles then returned to Kensington Palace for a stiff drink and the next day, he played polo – just as he had done after the birth of Prince William two years earlier.

Did You Know?

There were few celebrations after the birth of Princess Diana, a third daughter, on July 1 1961. Her parents, in particular her father John Spencer, Viscount Althorp, were devastated she was not a boy. They had lost a newborn son within hours of his birth the year before and were desperate for a male heir. Diana's father was (wrongly) convinced that fault lay with his wife and he sent her to Harley Street for medical tests to investigate why she only seemed able to bear healthy girl children.

SUGAR DADDIES

In recent years the phenomenon that is the 'Push Present' or 'Baby Bauble' - a very sparkly, very expensive gift bestowed on a new mother by her grateful partner on the birth of their child – has gained momentum in the UK and the USA. More and more 'sugar daddies' have followed the lead set by stars such as former James Bond actor Pierce Brosnan who presented his wife, Keeley, with three gold-and-diamond bracelets on the birth of their first son. However the 'Push Present' has its origins in the Royal Courts of Europe. There could be no more grateful a new father than a Prince or King desperate for a healthy heir to continue his dynastic line. And like today's A-listers, Royalty has always had great wealth at its disposal with which to purchase a premier 'Push Pressie'. New daddy Will is reported to be looking through his late mother's extensive jewellery collection in order to find the perfect 'Push Present' for new mummy Kate. But what have other Royal Ladies received, having successfully produced an heir - or spare?

Eleanor of Provence. Henry III ordered a complete makeover of his wife Eleanor's chamber in Westminster Palace following the birth of son and heir Prince

Edward on June 16 1239. The fashion-conscious, trend-setting Queen (she wore tight-fitting gowns of scarlet damask and introduced the cone-like Wimple head dress to England) was rewarded with a freshly green-painted wainscot (wood panelling) decorated with gold stars.

Isabella of France. Having given birth to Edward II's son and heir, the future Edward III, on November 13 1312, the King presented his wife with the Manor of Macclesfield in Cheshire but he was also extremely generous towards the Queen's squire who brought him news of the birth – a payment of £20 (worth approximately £5600 today) in addition to a life pension of £80 (£22,400). When their second son, John, was born on August 15 1316, Edward rewarded the messenger who brought him the news with £100 (£28,000) but also provided the Queen's tailor with six pieces of white velvet for her churching robe. He gifted Isabella with jewellery, lands and cloth for new corsets. But maybe these were more 'guilt gifts' than 'push presents'. Edward II had a habit of falling in love with his male courtiers.

Jane Seymour. Henry VIII was spoiling his third wife even before she gave birth to his longed-for son and heir, Edward, on October 12 1537. He bought her *a great, rich bed* with a gilt bed-head some months earlier. Not exactly imaginative with a pressie, he had also bought splendid beds of state for Catherine of Aragon and Anne Boleyn to labour on.

Queen Elizabeth II. Following the birth of Prince Charles on November 14 1948, Prince Philip presented his wife, then Princess Elizabeth, with a bottle of champagne and a big bouquet of her favourite flowers – camellias, lilies, carnations and roses - purchased, incidentally, by his equerry.

Princess Diana. A fantastic haul for Diana when Prince William was born on June 21 1982! New dad Charles presented her with a necklace of diamonds and cultured pearls with a sparkling heart at the centre. He also bought her a solid gold 'W' for her charm bracelet as well as a brand new, custom-built mini in apple green with a convertible foldaway roof and enough space for a collapsible cot.

Crown Princess Mary of Denmark. It's customary for the Royal Ladies of Denmark to receive sapphire jewellery on the birth of a child. True to tradition, when the Australian-born Mary gave birth to Princess Isabella on 21 April 2007, her husband Frederik presented her with a pendant of light blue and pink sapphires.

Did You Know?

Napoleon may have been poorly endowed and obsessed with his 'moobs' (man boobs) but what a very generous new daddy he was. When his former mistress Marie Waleswska gave birth to his son Alexandre on May 4 1810, he sent her a gift of Brussels lace, had her Parisian house redecorated and refurbished, bought her a holiday home in Boulogne, provided her with free tickets to the Parisian theatres, free entry to all the museums and galleries plus a monthly allowance of 10,000 francs (around £50,000 today). No wonder she didn't mind being sidelined.

IV

Blue Blooded Babies

———

*'Thank God he doesn't have his
father's ears'*

Queen Elizabeth II on seeing grandson Prince
William for the first time.

Royal births may be accompanied by military gun salutes and the posting of framed notices on Palace gates but the newborns themselves are, of course, just like any other babies. They sleep, eat, poop, pee, cry, squirm, scream, wriggle – and then they do it all over again. Just as customs, fashions, habits and traditions of pregnancy and birth have changed over the centuries, so has the way in which we – and indeed the Royal 'We' – care for our newborns. For hundreds of years, new baby Royals were handed over to wet-nurses to breastfeed them as soon as they were born. Then there was the dry-nurse, five or six 'rockers' of the Royal cradle and an omnipresent laundress to wash the never-ending pile of soiled linen napkins and the like. Tiny Princes and Princesses had their own little Kingdoms or 'Nursery Palaces', sometimes miles away from their parents' court - with a visit on only special occasions. The future Elizabeth I, for instance, was provided with her own household at Hatfield when she was just three-months-old. From then on, her mother, Anne Boleyn, could do little for her daughter apart from providing Elizabeth with pretty clothes in the best fabrics, and elaborate furnishings. By Victorian times, Royal babies saw more of their nannies and servants than their parents, but at least they lived within the same four walls. Queen Alexandra, when

Princess of Wales, was regarded as unusual because she visited the nursery every morning and evening, and often bathed her babies herself – *'She was in her glory when she could run up to the nursery, put on a flannel apron, wash the children herself and see them asleep in their little beds'.* It wasn't until over a century later that another Royal mother, Diana, adopted a similar hands-on approach with her babies, although her sons, William and Harry, were still products of an upper class nanny state. Baby Cambridge, however, is being raised the middle class, Middleton way – just as Kate was herself.

Did You Know?

As new parents Prince and Princess Michael of Kent weren't exactly hands-on. One evening in 1980 when their son, Lord Frederick Windsor, was a baby, they reportedly asked the Royal Protection Squad to locate his nanny who was having a night off. Little Freddie had woken up crying and his panicky parents had stood outside his nursery, not knowing what to do.

A WEIGHTY ISSUE

In Royal circles, the weight of a newborn baby wasn't usually recorded in terms of pounds and ounces until the end of the nineteenth century. On the day of her birth in May 1819 Queen Victoria was described as a '*pocket Hercules*' by her proud father, the Duke of Kent - so we can presume she was no underweight weakling. Similarly when her cousin, Princess Charlotte of Wales, was born 22 years earlier, her father, the future George IV, wrote that his new daughter was '*immense*'. Precise weights and measures tended to be recorded when a baby was premature, such as Prince Albert Victor, eldest son of the future Edward VII and therefore heir to the British throne. He tops our chart as the tiniest Royal baby to survive.

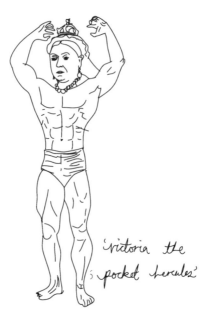

'victoria the
'pocket hercules'

Prince Albert Victor   3lbs 3¾ oz, born two months prematurely on January 8 1864.

Lady Louise Windsor   4lbs 9oz, born a month prematurely on November 8 2003.

Prince Edward   5lb 7oz, born a week early on March 10 1964.

Princess Anne   6lbs, born August 15 1950.

Prince Harry   6lbs 14oz, born September 15 1984.

Prince William   7lbs 1½ oz, born June 21 1982, induced a week early.

Prince Charles   7lbs 6oz, born November 14 1948.

Diana   7lbs 12oz, born July 1 1961.

Duke of Windsor   8lbs, born June 24 1894.

Zara Phillips   8lbs 1oz, born May 15 1981.

James Ogilvy, son of Princess Alexandra   9lbs 6oz, born February 29 1964.

Did You Know?

Queen Victoria, believing she was a descendent of King David, sanctioned the circumcision of her baby sons. From Edward VII onwards, all male Royalty were given the snip. Prince Charles was circumcised by a 'mohel' (a Jewish person specialising in circumcision) who was chosen over the Royal physician. Rabbi Jacob Snowman performed the procedure at Buckingham Palace in 1948, five days after the Prince's christening. However, Princes William and Harry were not circumcised. Diana vetoed the idea, breaking a tradition that dated back to the 1840s.

To Feed or not to Feed?

Elizabeth II breastfed all four of her children, Diana fed William and Harry for two months a-piece, Kate is also breastfeeding baby Cambridge – or certainly intends to. But from a historical perspective, this is a relatively recent phenomenon. From Ancient Egyptian to Victorian times, Royal mothers rarely breastfed their offspring. A woman who breastfeeds full time neither ovulates nor menstruates, and therefore cannot get pregnant. As it was the duty, indeed purpose, of a Royal Wife to provide an heir and several spares, she would be bidden to get to back to baby-making as soon as possible. There were also social and aesthetic reasons why Royal Mothers chose not to breastfeed. Great ladies did not nurse their own children because it was considered animalistic and vulgar. Breastfeeding was also considered to ruin the shape of the bosom and the philandering French King Louis XV openly disliked the practice for this reason. Royal newborns would be put to the breast of a wet-nurse, a woman who had already given birth to her own child and was therefore capable of feeding others, as soon as they were born. Some Royal mothers in history bucked this trend – or at least wanted to – while others were appalled at the very notion of feeding their own babies. . .

It is said that **Anne Boleyn** wanted to go against tradition and breastfeed her baby daughter, the future Elizabeth I, herself. She was, however, prevented from doing so. It was unthinkable for a woman of Anne's status to feed her child when a wet-nurse could be employed. Henry VIII refused to let Anne breastfeed and not just because of his selfish desire for a good night's sleep or because it went against protocol. He was desperate to get Anne pregnant again so that she would finally give birth to a son. She did indeed fall pregnant again on at least two occasions but miscarried both times.

Marie Antoinette. From the off, she decided to take care of her children herself and, for 18 days, breastfed her daughter, Marie (born December 19 1778), an act that horrified many, including her mother, the Empress Maria Theresa. Upon hearing this news, the Empress sent a letter to her daughter, ordering her to cease such '*barbarism*', warning her that

let them drink my milk...

Marie Antoinette

breastfeeding would prevent her from getting pregnant again. Marie Antoinette dutifully obeyed her mama.

Queen Victoria's mother, **Victoire, Duchess of Kent**, was so elated to have given birth to little Alexandrina Victoria, as the baby was called, in May 1819, she made the unusual decision to feed the baby herself. *'I would have been desperate to see my little darling on someone else's breast,'* she wrote to her mother. *'Everybody was quite astonished.'* It is interesting to speculate that if Victoire hadn't made this unexpected break with precedence and had handed her daughter over to a wet-nurse, she may well have fallen pregnant again before the Duke's unexpected death in January 1820. If she had given birth to a son after Victoria, the *'pocket Hercules'* whose name encapsulated an age, would never have ascended the throne.

Queen Victoria inherited no such maternal feelings when her own nine children were born - anything but. She found breastfeeding to be a disgusting practice. *'The horror about that peculiarly indelicate nursing - which is far worse than all the other parts,'* she wrote. *'When one is high-born - one can avoid and ought to avoid. I maintain that a child can never be as well-nursed by a lady of rank and nervous and refined temperament - for the less* *feeling and the more like an animal the wet nurse is, the better for the child.'* Victoria was appalled when two of her daughters, Vicky and Alice, chose to breastfeed their own babies – although Vicky did not feed her three eldest children herself. Queen Victoria not only disapproved of Vicky nursing her younger babies but was furious at her for influencing younger sister Alice to nurse her newborn, too. The Queen had thought that Alice, like herself, *'disliked the disgusting details of the nursery...all and every one of which Vicky delights in'* and was pained to discover otherwise. *'There is in everything the animal side of our nature but it hurts me deeply that my own two daughters should set at defiance the advice of a Mother of 9 children, 46 years old. It does make my hair stand on end to think that my two daughters should turn into cows.'* Victoria duly named cows in the Royal dairy after her daughters. Vicky actually breast-fed Alice's son, Frittie (born October 7 1870) but neither daughter chose to tell their mother.

The ill-fated **Tsarina Alexandra Feodorovna of Russia** tried to breastfeed her first daughter Olga, born November 15 1895, but one of the first attempts ended with the Tsarina breastfeeding the son of the wet-nurse and the wet-nurse feeding Olga!

> *Did You Know?*
>
> ---
>
> In 1103, Sybilla of Conversano, William the
> Conqueror's eldest daughter-in law, is said to
> have died from an infection brought on by the
> binding of her breasts after childbirth.

—

THE ROLE OF THE ROYAL WET-NURSE

Becoming the wet-nurse of a Royal baby was considered a great honour. Women lucky enough to become Royal wet-nurses in Ancient Egypt, for instance, were honoured in the tombs of their charges. In addition to this, their own children were raised in the Royal Palace as 'milk siblings' of the Princes and Princesses with whom they experienced close relationships. It could also be a lucrative profession. Mrs Muttlebury, the wet-nurse employed by Queen Charlotte, wife of George III, to feed her eldest daughter Charlotte, Princess Royal in 1766, was paid £200 (around £17,000 today) a year while on milk duty, and when her employment ceased, received a pension of £100 a year for the rest of her life. At a time when women had very little earning power, this was a respectable wage. When a Royal Lady was expecting a child, several wet-nurses would be kept 'on standby' and the new Prince or Princess may have had several wet -nurses until weaning. French King Louis XVI (born August 23 1754), for instance, had four wet-nurses before he was weaned at the age of two. What qualities were required in a wet-nurse? The ideal medieval model was a young woman with a pink and white complexion. Red-headed wet-nurses were avoided because it was thought that babies absorbed the characteristics of the woman nursing them – and red-heads were thought to have legendary tempers. Interestingly this changed during the Tudor period, the Tudors themselves being tawny-headed. By Stuart times, the red-headed, freckled wet-nurse had fallen out of favour once more - it was thought her milk would be sour in addition to fiery. A healthy 'brown' complexion was preferred and stayed in vogue for the next 200 years - according to Queen Victoria the perfect nineteenth century wet-nurse was *very dark and thin and with plenty of milk.* A wet-nurse was thought to pass on her own characteristics to a child through her milk, so her diet was needed to be good and wholesome, without too much garlic or strongly flavoured foods. She should also be of a good, placid nature and healthy appearance, with clear skin and no visible afflictions. In Royal households, tasters were appointed to check her food was neither poisoned nor too strong.

Tutankamum's wet-nurse, ***Maia*** or ***Matia***, is known from her rock-cut tomb found at Saqqara in Eqypt. Maia bears the titles '*wet nurse of the King, educator of the god's body and great one of the harim.*' In the tomb, Tutankhamun is shown sitting on Maia's lap and the King is mentioned several times in the inscriptions.

Welsh woman ***Mariota Maunsel*** was ***King Edward II's*** wet-nurse for the first few months of his life in 1284, until she fell ill and had to leave his household. In November 1307, Edward gave Mariota 73 acres of land in Caernarfon, rent-free for life. Mariota was replaced as Edward's nurse by English woman, ***Alice de Leygrave***, who in May 1313 was called '*the king's mother...who suckled him in his youth*'.

Anne Launcelyn was appointed wet-nurse to the infant ***Henry Tudor*** (later Henry VIII). She lived primarily at Eltham Palace, where the Royal nursery was located, but the downside of her job was that she had to live chastely and was held responsible for any ill-health the baby suffered. If he had colic, she was purged. If her milk supply was inadequate, she was made to eat stewed udders of goats or sheep, or powdered earthworms, since these 'cures' were supposed to produce more milk. It's not known what Anne looked like but Tudor physicians believed a wet-nurse should have '*rosy cheeks, a white skin, thick reddish hair, a fleshy body and a hopeful, brave, amorous disposition . . . a thick neck, broad breasts and be aged about 25, of a respectable status if not actually a gentlewoman, and without vice.*' It is likely that Anne remained at Eltham until Henry was seven-years-old and she may also have been one of Catherine of Aragon's chamber women. She was certainly present at Henry's Coronation in 1509.

Christabella Wyndham was the wet-nurse of the baby **Charles II**. But that's not all she was. It was Christabella who introduced Charles to '*that little fantastical man called Cupid*', as he later put it. She seduced him and took his virginity when he was 15! His advisor Edward Hyde was shocked, noting that Christabella, who was the wife of the royalist Governor of Bridgewater, was '*a woman of great rudeness and country pride*'.

A **Mrs Pack** was a wet-nurse to **William, Duke of Gloucester**, the only surviving child of the future Queen Anne, who was born July 24 1689. Three other wet-nurses had tried and failed to suckle the newborn. He was ailing so a call went out from Hampton Court for suitable women to come forward. Among them was Mrs. Pack, a Quaker from Kingston Wick. As she sat in the Presence Room nursing her own month-old baby, Prince George of Denmark, Princess Anne's husband and father of the Duke, passed through the room and noticed Mrs. Pack because of '*her breasts, which were gigantic*'. He ordered Mrs. Pack to go to his son and feed him. She did so and the baby recovered. Mrs Pack went on to wield great power within the household but she never won the affection of William. She died in 1694 but when the five-year-old-boy was asked if he was sad, he replied that he was not. Six years later, William had perished, too.

The aforementioned **Louis XVI** had trouble with his wet-nurses from the start. His primary wet-nurse did not have enough milk. This should not have been problematic as six reserve wet-nurses were ready and waiting to take over. However the unsatisfactory wet-nurse remained in her post. Eventually it transpired that she was the mistress of the Minister of the Household, the Comte de Saint-Florentin, and he was loathe to fire her. All was well in the end. Saint-Florentin's subterfuge was discovered, the lady was dismissed from Versailles and replaced one of the reserve wet-nurses.

The baby *Marie Antoinette* (born November 2 1755) was taken care of by wet-nurse, **Constance Weber.** When Marie Antoinette was a child, she often gave gifts to Constance and her son, Joseph, whom Marie Antoinette regarded as a 'foster' brother as they had suckled from the same breast. According to Joseph, Marie Antoinette once said to Constance, *'Good Weber, have a care for your son.'* Joseph also reported that the little Archdukes and Archduchesses of the Austrian Court were allowed to make friends with 'ordinary' children. Apart from formal celebration days, lowborns who were liked were allowed into court.

Mrs Muttleberry, the wet-nurse of *Princess Charlotte, Princess Royal,* was carefully vetted before she took up her appointment in autumn 1766. She had to be approved by Lady Charlotte Finch - the head of the Royal Nursery, in addition to a doctor and two surgeons. The baby she had been suckling and her elder child were brought in for inspection to show that both thrived. When she was accepted as wet-nurse, Mrs Muttleberry had to devote herself to six months unconditional feeding of the little Princess. She was allowed no visitors, not even her own children, in case they distracted her. She was also ordered to wear silks, brocade and finest lace to ensure that the Royal baby came into contact with superior fabrics, only!

Queen Victoria's eldest child, *Vicky*, was three weeks premature when she was born at Buckingham Palace on November 21 1840. The wet-nurse who had been selected for her was a doctor's wife living on the Isle of Wight and as the baby was premature, she was sent for early and forced to cross the English Channel in an open boat. The rules of the Royal nursery were so strict, Vicky's wet-nurse had to stand while feeding her.

Puyi, the last Chinese Emperor born on February 7 1906, became Emperor when he was just two-years-old. He was not to see his biological mother, Princess Consort Chun, for the next seven years, and developed a special bond with his wet-nurse, Wen-Chao Wang. He later credited her with being the only person able to control him. She was sent away when he was eight-years-old but when he had grown up, she would sometimes visit him in the Forbidden City. Throughout Chinese history, suppliers for the Forbidden City lived in neighbourhoods outside its walls. One was known as 'Wet-Nurse Lane' as it was inhabited by wet-nurses recruited from all over China in order to breastfeed the babies of the Imperial nursery.

Did You Know?

On leaving Royal service, a Mrs Brough, Edward VII's wet-nurse, went on to become a murderess! In 1855, following a quarrel with her husband, she slit the throats of her own six children before trying to kill herself. She was detained at a mental institution for the rest of her life.

Nanny Knows Best

After the wet-nurses and the weaning came the nanny – arguably the most important person in the Royal Baby's life. When Royal parents only saw their offspring for an hour or so a day, it was nanny who did the child-rearing – the feeding, bathing, changing, disciplining, hugging, playing and general looking-after-of. It has been reported that while Queen Elizabeth II would sometimes go up to the nursery and watch her children being bathed, she never got her own hands wet. Even hands-on Royal mothers like Princess Diana didn't do much of the nuts-and-bolts, nappy changing stuff. She would bath her babies and read to them when they were older and when time allowed – ditto Prince Charles - but it was nanny who slept upstairs in the nursery in the room next to Wills and Harry, nanny who generally got them up in the morning and breakfasted with them. Aristocrat Diana, had, of course, been raised by nannies herself so this probably seemed normal. But Kate's babyhood was very different. It was mother Carole who raised her own three babies – Kate, Pippa and James - and who now, as a grandmother, is delighted to be doing her bit. The nanny employed by the Cambridges is likely to be part-time as Kate and William, aided by the 'uber-capable' Carole, wish to do as much of the child rearing as possible. For baby Cambridge, it won't be Nanny but Granny who knows best.

'Roosie'. Nanny Roose. ***Prince Philip's*** nanny, raised his mother before him and was undoubtedly the greatest influence in his early life. His parents' marriage was unhappy and the family had no settled home so it was Nanny Roose who provided continuity and security. Before Philip's birth in June 1921, Nanny Roose ordered supplies of British soap, British baby food and British woolies to be delivered to Corfu. She taught Philip English nursery rhymes and, although money was tight, dressed him in clothes sent from England. She insisted he speak English and observe English customs. She had her work cut out as he was a rascal. One of his favourite tricks was escaping from 'Roosie' at bath time. He would run naked through the halls of whatever castle the family happened to be staying in at the time until someone finally caught him and brought him back to the bathtub.

Clara Knight. This strict-but-fair Hertfordshire-born nanny had looked after Lady Elizabeth Bowes Lyon as a baby before Elizabeth, as Duchess of York, employed her to tend to the new-born, future Elizabeth II, in

1926. This practice of passing-down-the-nanny was very common amongst the British upper classes, had been for years and would be for many more to come. Known as 'Alah' – her young charges could never get their tongues around 'Clara' – she ruled the nursery, the nursery footmen and assistants. Her word was law. The Duchess gave her complete control with the result that baby Elizabeth, who was always dressed in hand-stitched garments of white cotton, was raised in the same time-honoured way her mother had been. 'Alah' believed in neither pandering to nor pampering 'her' children. She and Elizabeth lived in a suite of *'sunny'* rooms at the top of Yorks' house in Mayfair, London, which consisted of a day nursery, night nursery and bathroom linked by a landing with wide windows which looked down on the park. It was a loving and calm yet neat and ordered environment, and discipline was the order of the day. A strict routine was adhered to at all times with routine periods set aside for feeding, bathing, playing and parental visits. It was 'Alah' who took care of Elizabeth when her parents toured Australasia for six months when she was only nine-months-old. It was 'Alah' 15-month-old Elizabeth clung to when her parents returned. Also omnipresent in this cloistered world was 'Alah's' nursery assistant, Margaret McDonald, whom Elizabeth named 'Bobo' and who became the future Queen's dresser and most trusted companion until her death at the age of 89 in 1993.

Helen Lightbody. A Royal nanny in the 'Alah/Bobo' mold, this Scottish-born daughter of an Edinburgh textile worker was known as 'no nonsense Lightbody', yet she was thought to have been very kind and fair. Originally the nanny of Princes William and Richard, the sons of the Queen's uncle, the Duke of Gloucester, she then ran the Buckingham Palace nursery from 1948, when Prince Charles was a month old, until she left in 1956. Charles adored her and his first word is thought to have been 'Nana', his name for her. It was 'Nana' who got Charles up in the morning and dressed him– just as 'Alah' had done with his mother. 'Nana' also slept in the same room as little Charles and comforted him when he awoke in the night. She left Royal service under something of a cloud – it's said the Queen fired her because she overruled a dessert Her Majesty had ordered for Prince Charles' dinner.

Mabel Anderson. 'No-nonsense Lightbody's' assistant, Mabel, a policeman's daughter from Elgin, Scotland, joined the Royal Household in 1949 as assistant nanny – the then Princess Elizabeth liked

Mabel's quiet, unassuming manner. Prince Charles described her as '*a haven of security, the greatest haven*' and so cherished her, he wanted her to come out of retirement and care for the newborn William in 1982. Diana, wishing to do things her own way, wouldn't entertain the idea. Mabel nannied all four of Elizabeth II's children and also helped to raise Peter Phillips, the son of Princess Anne, for the first two-and-a-half years of his life. She was called upon by Prince Charles to comfort him and his sons after Diana was killed in 1997. Two years later, she joined Charles on a cruise on a yacht owned by the Greek billionaire John Latsis. Now 86, she retains a grace-and-favour apartment

Mabel & Camilla

near Windsor Castle. Each Christmas, Charles sends a chauffeur-driven car to take Mabel to Sandringham, where she is treated like a cherished member of the family rather than an employee. Curiously, Mabel in her younger years is said to have resembled Camilla, and it has been suggested that this was the main reason Charles fell in love with his second wife!

June Waller. A young Lincolnshire girl who became Mabel's assistant after the birth of Prince Andrew, June's letters written to a friend, provide a tantalizing glimpse into life in the Buckingham Palace Nursery. *'Andrew has gorgeous fat little legs. Really he's a poppet. He's doing well and now weighs 9lb 9oz. He's on half-cream Cow & Gate (baby formula milk),'* she wrote. *'The other evening I had the Queen, Duke, Princess Royal (Elizabeth II's aunt), Duchess of Kent (Elizabeth II's aunt), Lady Brabourne (Patricia, Countess Mountbatten of Burma) and Lady Abergavenny (lady-in-waiting to the Queen) all sitting round the nursery fire watching me give Andrew his supper!! It was terrible. I should think I can face anything after that! I had to will myself not to let my hand shake!'* In September 1960, when Andrew was seven-months-old, June wrote from Balmoral, *'This morning he weighed 21lb 14oz. We have now run out of weights - next week we shall have to borrow from the kitchen! He cut another tooth today making seven and there is another one almost through. So by the 19th he should have eight teeth - which, according to all good books, is correct.'* In April 1962, she wrote, *'We had PM's (Princess Margaret's) nursery down to tea - they are staying [at Windsor Castle] until Tuesday, I believe. David Linley is rather sweet - but (his) nanny pampers him rather in our opinion, over-clothes him, too. Poor little brute. A gorgeous day, central heating and fire and he's wearing a woolly vest, usual nappies and waterproof pants, woolly pants on top of that, and a flannel petticoat plus ordinary petticoat and dress and socks and woolly shoes!! At five months! Oh, and I forgot, a great big shawl to take him along a centrally heated corridor - I ask you!'* **Nanny Sumner**, the nanny of Princess Margaret's two children, David and Sarah, did not get on with Mabel Anderson and her staff. *'There was a lot of tension between them,'* a former Royal servant once recalled. *'They were like two rival camps.'*

Barbara Barnes. Prince William's first nanny was also the first Royal nanny not to have at least two nursery footmen and nursemaids to help her. *'I am here to help, not to take over,'* she was quoted as saying shortly after her appointment in 1982. Prince

William came to so love 'Baba', he'd get into bed with her before most mornings before breakfast. There are conflicting rumours as to why Barbara left the Wales' employ in 1987 - Diana was jealous of her elder son's attachment to his Baba, Barbara became irritated when Diana constantly interfered in nursery life, the Queen suggested that a stricter nanny should be employed as William was becoming a handful or simply because William had started school and Barbara felt it was time to move on. Whatever the reason, 'Baba' remains very dear to William. She was one of the first people he invited to his wedding.

When Nanny Didn't Know Best. . .

One Royal nanny had a far from positive effect on her charges.

Nanny Green was not a well woman when she was appointed to look after the very young children of the future George V and Queen Mary in the 1890s. Mentally unbalanced, she loved David, the future Edward VIII, with a sadistic obsession. She did not wish to share him with anyone, not even his own parents. When it was time to take David in to see his mother and father each afternoon, she would pinch and jab him until he cried. Mary and George were clueless when it came to parenting. They did not want to deal with a crying baby and would order him to be removed. The nanny would then cuddle and soothe David until he was all better. While she adored David, Nanny Green neglected his younger brother, Bertie, the future George VI. Sometimes she forgot to feed him, at other times she would give him his bottle while he was in his baby carriage and riding over rough cobblestones, which would result in a severely tummy upset. Finally, a nursery maid called Mrs Bill, fearing Nanny Green would kill Bertie, managed to get up enough courage to tell his mother what was happening. Nanny Green was duly sacked and Mrs Bill, known affectionately as 'Lalla', was appointed in her place.

Did You Know?

When Eleanor, the eldest child of Joanna of Castile and Philip the Handsome, was born on 15 November 1498, Philip refused to pay for the upkeep of the nursery because Joanna had given birth to a girl. He maintained the infant's care should be his wife's responsibility. *'Because this child is a girl, let the Archduchess provide the estate,'* he said, *'and then when God grants us a son, I will provide it.'*

'Abandoned' Royal Babies

It is quite unthinkable now but for hundreds of years, Royalty thought nothing of leaving their young offspring for weeks, months, even years on end. While it was protocol for Norman, Plantagenet and Tudor Monarchs to set up separate households for their little ones, some took this separation to extremes. Edward I and Eleanor of Castile, for instance, voluntarily left England for Gascony in May 1286 when their youngest son, Edward of Caernarfon, was just two-years-old, and they didn't return until he was five! Some later monarchs chose to be almost as distant. When he was a baby, Queen Victoria's fourth son, the haemophiliac Leopold, was left for months on end in the total care of his Scottish wet-nurse. When long visits to far-flung places became de-rigeur for Royals, there was never any question of taking a baby along. Queen Victoria refused to give her daughter-in-law, Princess Alexandra, permission to take her new baby daughter, Victoria (born July 6 1868), to visit her parents in Denmark in the late autumn of that year. Victoria only allowed the 20-month-old, elder daughter, Louise, to go after pleading letters had been sent from Alexandra and Bertie, the future Edward VIII. As the couple then left Denmark in January 1869 to embark on a six month trip to Egypt – little Louise and her two older brothers, the future George V and the future Duke of Clarence, having travelled back to England – they did not see baby Victoria for seven months. Returning from her travels, Alexandra was overjoyed to be reunited with her children again – as indeed were the children who had not enjoyed staying with their strict grandmother. Interestingly Alexandra's own grandchildren, the future Edward VIII, George VI and their siblings, were delighted when their strict, discplinarian parents - the future George V and Queen Mary - left them with their far more easy-going grandparents for eight months in August 1900 in order to visit Australia. With such a strong tradition of Royal parents leaving their children and babies in the care of others, it is perhaps not surprising that the practice carried on for many more years to come. 'Loneliness is something Royal children have always suffered and always will,' said the late, semi-Royal Lord Louis Mountbatten. 'Not much you can do about it really.' New mummy Cambridge would not agree.

As a nine-month-old baby, **Elizabeth II** was left with her grandparents, George V and Queen Mary, as her parents, the then Duke and Duchess of York, visited Australasia for six months. Her mother, the former

Lady Elizabeth Bowes Lyons, was particularly upset at the parting in January 1927. *'Feeling very miserable at leaving the baby,'* she wrote on the morning of departure. *'Went up and played with her and she was so sweet. Luckily she doesn't realize anything.'* Once she'd departed, the Duchess *'drank some champagne and tried not to weep'*. It is an indication of the times that rather than criticizing the Duchess for leaving her baby for so long, the newspapers of the day applauded her sense of duty. Baby Elizabeth's nanny, Clare 'Alah' Knight patiently taught her to say the word 'Mummy'. Since, however, there was nobody to whom the word could be accurately applied, Elizabeth greeted everybody she came across, including family portraits, with *'Mummy, Mummy!'* Did 15-month-old Elizabeth recognize her mother when she returned? Sadly not. The little girl burst into tears and refused to go into her mother's arms. She clung to her nanny's skirt before she could be persuaded to join the Royal Family on the balcony of Buckingham Palace.

Once she had become a mother herself, **Princess – then Queen – Elizabeth** also left her children, particularly the elder two, for long periods of time. Given the kind of upbringing she had herself had, it's not surprising that she and Prince Philip left their children in order to go on lengthy Royal tours. But what is unusual is the fact that she chose not to take her babies with her on the two separate occasions, before she became Queen, when she lived the life of a Navy wife in Malta. In 1949 she spent several weeks on the island with Philip, both parents missing Charles' first birthday, his first tooth and first step. They didn't return for Christmas or when he was ill with tonsillitis. Princess Anne was born on August 15 1950 but as soon as Princess Elizabeth had finished breastfeeding when Anne was three-months old, she flew out to Malta to spend extended time, again 'sans enfants', with her beloved Philip.

Only seven weeks after the birth of her first baby, David Viscount Linley in November 1961, the late **Princess Margaret** and her then husband, Lord Snowdon, left baby David in London while they holidayed

in Antigua in the Caribbean. One British newspaper called Margaret '*callous*' for leaving the baby behind but she was only doing what Royals had done for centuries. The arrival of baby girl, Sarah, in May 1964 didn't change the Snowdons' ways. Every summer, they'd party in Europe with their smart friends while the children stayed at Balmoral with Nanny Sumner.

In autumn 1988 **Sarah, Duchess of York** was lambasted for leaving her new baby daughter, Beatrice, at home while she joined her then-sailor, then-husband, Prince Andrew, in Australia. This was no longer acceptable and the decision to leave her baby behind, albeit with nanny Alison Wardley and Prince Andrew's old nanny Mabel Anderson, saw Sarah being widely criticized. The Duchess' defense? '*I thought it was more important to be with my husband,*' she said. '*It was his turn and I think that was the right thing to have done.*' Unfortunately, public opinion wasn't with her.

It was **Princess Diana** who famously bucked the trend of leaving the children at home when Royal duty – or pleasure - called overseas. But actually it wasn't Diana who insisted that eight-month-old Prince William accompany her and Prince Charles when they toured

Australia and New Zealand for six weeks in early 1983. *'I was all ready to leave William,'* Diana wrote. *'I accepted that as part of duty, albeit that it wasn't going to be easy.'* Malcolm Fraser, Australian Prime Minister at the time, wrote to the Princess, suggesting that she and Prince Charles bring William with them. *'It was wonderful,'* Diana commented. *'We didn't see very much of him but at least we were under the same sky, so to speak.'* When William and Harry were small, Diana would refuse to go on tour for more than three weeks at a time and always made time for at least one daily call home whenever she was on the road.

Did You Know?

Before Henry VIII decreed that the three-month-old Elizabeth I be moved to her own 'Nursery Palace' at Hatfield in December 1533, her mother Anne Boleyn refused to be parted from her. Baby Elizabeth would lie on a velvet cushion next to her mother's throne. It was highly unusual for a Queen to keep her child with her but Anne, always unconventional, insisted.

Prams By Royal Appointment

English garden architect William Kent is credited with developing the first known pram. In 1733, the Duke of Devonshire asked Kent to build a means of transportation that would carry his children. Kent obliged by constructing a shell-shaped basket-on-wheels in which the children could sit. It was designed with a harness so that an animal such as a goat or pony could pull it, and was also designed with springs so the Duke's children could ride in comfort. Kent's 'baby carriage' was a great success and it became an essential purchase for the well-to-do parent. In the years that followed, several important design changes were made to the style of the carriage. Most importantly, they were equipped with a handle rather a harness which meant the emphasis was on convenience for nannies and, occasionally mothers, rather than for the amusement of children. In the 1840s, the baby carriage had its first 'big break' when Queen Victoria bought three 'push-style' ones. Since those days, there has been a very special relationship between certain Royal Babies and certain brands of perambulator. . .

The three, ready-made baby carriages **Queen Victoria** acquired were designed to perambulate toddlers who could sit up and take an interest in the world. Purchased from '**Hitchings of Ludgate Hill**' in London, they were large, high-backed vehicles that weren't especially safe. Nevertheless, the **Spanish** and **Egyptian Royal Families** promptly purchased Hitchings prams for their offspring, too. It is interesting to note that when the first 'push-style' prams and baby carriages appeared in the late nineteenth century, they were banned from public footpaths like other four wheel

vehicles. Several women were prosecuted for pushing their babies on these public walking areas, but the law eventually decided that mothers with baby carriages didn't pose much of a safety risk.

The iconic **Silver Cross** pram company supplied little **Princess Elizabeth's** first baby carriage in 1926. The company was founded in 1877 by William Wilson, a former postman, from Leeds. He set up his first workshop in Silver Cross Street in the nearby village of Hunslet in order to manufacture perambulators with a unique design of folding hood and heavy spring suspension. By 1897, the company had grown to the extent that new premises were required and the 'Silver Cross Works' were completed on White House Street. The company was awarded a Royal warrant before Wilson's death in 1913. **Princess Grace of Monaco** used a Silver Cross pram for her three children while **Princess Diana** was also pushed around in one as a baby - her first memory being, '*really the inside of my pram, it was plastic, and the smell of the hood*'. In 1977, Silver Cross presented **Princess Anne** with a special model for her newborn, **Peter Phillips**. It's thought that as newborns, **Princes William** and **Harry** were also pushed around in a Silver Cross. **Carole Middleton** was another 'Silver Cross' baby. Her mother Dorothy Goldsmith, known as 'Lady Dorothy' for her airs and graces, took great delight in showing off baby Carole in her posh SC pram.

It is a common misconception that **Queen Elizabeth** II used Silver Cross prams for her babies. Not so. She used a **Millson** pram - a classic hand-built luxury baby carriage, a Millson Twin Cavendish adapted for single use. Silver Cross did, however, restore the trusty Millson for Prince Edward as the latter company ceased trading in 1960s.

The must-have buggy/stroller for the 1980s Royal baby was the lightweight, foldaway **Maclaren** 'Umbrella' type model. **Princes William** and **Harry** were occasionally seen being pushed around Kensington Gardens in a Maclaren by their nannies.

The Queen's eldest grandson, **Peter Phillips**, and his wife Autumn chose a **Phil & Teds Vibe** to push daughter Savannah around in. Phil & Teds Vibe has fast become a must-have pushchair and the choice for many a celebrity child in 2012/13.

Baby Cambridge, it is rumoured, has a very trendy designer Bugaboo baby carriage in which to be pushed around Kensington Gardens. Mother, **Kate Middleton**, is thought to have told army wives of her purchase during her pregnancy. The Bugaboo range is also a celebrity baby favourite – the Beckhams, the

Furnish-Johns and Sienna Miller have all chosen the brand for their babies.

Did You Know?

———————

Pram manufacturers have a tradition of labelling their ranges with names such as 'Queen', 'Princess', 'Royal' and 'Duchess', in order to exploit people's snobbery and the high hopes they naturally entertain for their children. The most popular names have been those of Royal residences, like 'Sandringham', 'Windsor' and 'Balmoral' - names which might suggest to parents that their sons and daughters were receiving the same start in life as the baby Prince and Princesses of the realm. The Silver Cross 'Balmoral' and 'Kensington' prams are still in production today.

V

Name that Royal

'I am very anxious to call her Anne as I think Anne of York sounds so pretty. Lots of people have suggested Margaret but it has no family links on either side and besides she will always be getting mixed up with Margaret the nursery maid'

Elizabeth, Duchess of York (later the Queen Mother) in a letter to in-laws King George V and Queen Mary after the birth of her second daughter in August 1930.

The Duchess may have thought Anne of York sounded '*so pretty*' but her father-in-law most definitely did not. He thought it a '*most unsuitable name*' and, being King, he had the final say. So, nursery maid or no nursery maid, the new HRH was named Margaret but with a 'Rose' attached to make it more fragrant and less servant-like. Naming a baby can be difficult enough but when you're a major Royal and your baby's next-in-line to the throne, you can't follow the celebrity route and come up with something wild, wacky or just plain silly. Princess Anne – the name finally found its way into 'the Firm' - called her daughter Zara but she knew there was very little chance of the girl ever becoming 'Queen Zara'. Tradition and protocol have always been of utmost importance to the leading Royals – with names as with everything else – and that is not going to change anytime soon.

Did You Know?

In August 1988, Prince Andrew and his then wife Sarah wanted to name their first born daughter 'Annabel' but the Queen vetoed the idea thinking the baby, at sixth in line, was too close to the throne to have such a non-royal name. Her Majesty can't have known that a 11th century Scottish Princess was named 'Amabel'. So the Victorian-influenced 'Beatrice' was chosen instead.

KEEPING IT IN THE FAMILY.

Christian names are endlessly recycled in Royal families – think 'Louis' in France and 'Henry' in Britain. Some names have figured in British Royal Dynasties for centuries. Saxon Kings bore the name of Edward over a millennia ago, for instance, yet the present Queen's youngest son also answers to it. Other names have gone in and out of Royal fashion. A daughter of Henry III was named Beatrice after her birth on June 25 1242, also a daughter of Edward born in 1286, but the name fell out of favour until Queen Victoria named her ninth child Beatrice in April 1857. It was resurrected again in August 1988 when the eldest daughter of the present Duke of York was born. Many historic 'Royal' names have fallen into disuse but maybe it's time to re-cycle some of them for a new generation of Royal babies. . .

SAXON AND VIKING NAMES PRE 1066

Female

Alstrita	A Devon-born noblewoman who married King Edgar in 964.
Astrid	Born in 997, a daughter of King Sweyn of Denmark who usurped the English throne in 1013.
Christina	A daughter of King Edmund II, born circa 1060.
Cyrid	The mother of King Sweyn.
Emma	Daughter of the Duke of Normandy, born between 985-7, who married King Ethelred II.
Thyra	Another daughter of King Sweyn born in 993.

Male

Alfred	Known as 'The Great', born between 846-9.
Athelstan	The first King of a united England, born 895.
Edmund	Known as 'The Magnificent' and Athelstan's half brother, born between 920-22. The name fell out of favour in the sixteenth century.
Harold	The most famous Saxon Harold was born between 1020-22 and killed at the Battle of Hastings in 1066.

NORMAN (1066-1154)

Female

Adela	The mother of King Stephen, born 1062.
Adeliza	A sister of William I, born 1029; a daughter of William I, born 1055; also the name Henry I's second wife's name, born between 1103-06.
Arlette	The mother of William I, born 1012.
Cecilia	A daughter of William I, born 1054/5.
Constance	A daughter of William I, born 1057 or 1061.
Eleanor	A sister of King Stephen, birth date not known. Famous later Royal Eleanors include Eleanor of Aquitaine, Henry II's Queen, born between 1120-22; Eleanor of Provence, Henry III's queen, born between circa 1223; and Eleanor of Castile, Edward I's Queen, born 1241.
Euphemia	A daughter of Henry I, born 1101.
Isabella	A grand daughter of King Stephen, birth date unknown. Famous later Royal Isabella's include Isabella of Angouleme, King John's Queen and second wife, born 1137; and Isabella 'She-wolf' of France, Edward II's Queen, who was born between 1292-95 and plotted her husband's downfall.
Matilda	The wife of William I, born 1029; the daughter and rightful heir of Henry 1, born 1080. Also a daughter of King Stephen, born 1133.

Male

Eustace	A son of King Stephen, born between 1127-31.
Robert	Eldest son of William I, born between 1052-4, who succeeded his father as Duke of Normandy.

PLANTAGENET (1154-1485)

Female

Berengaria	Spanish-born Queen of Richard I, born between 1163-5.
Blanche	Blanche of Lancaster, first wife of John of Gaunt and mother of Henry IV, born March 23 1345.
Bridget	Daughter of Edward IV, born November 10 1480, who became a nun.
Cecily	Edward IV's mother, born May 3 1415. Also a daughter of Edward IV, born March 20 1469.
Joanna	Also known as Joan, the daughter of Edward III and Queen Philippa, born December 19 1333.
Philippa	Edward III's queen, born 1313 or 14.

Male

Alfonso	Son of Edward I, born November 24 1273.
Geoffrey	The first Plantagenet, father of Henry II, born August 24 1113.
Thomas	13th child of Edward III and Queen Philippa, born January 7 1355.

TUDOR

Male

Jasper	Henry VII's uncle and Henry VI's half brother, born 1431.
Arthur	Eldest son of Henry VII, named to emphasize the new Tudor dynasty's links with the Kings of Ancient Britain, born September 20 1486.

Stuart

Female

Henrietta — The first Christian name of Charles I's Queen Henrietta Maria, born 26 November 1609. Also first name of their youngest daughter, Henrietta-Anne, born 16 June 1644.

Male

Rupert — Grandson of James I, born December 17 1619.

Hanoverian

Female

Adelaide — William IV's Queen, born August 13 1792.

Amelia — Amelia, daughter of George II, born May 30 1711. Also Amelia, the last and 15th child of George III, born August 7 1783.

Augusta — Mother of George III, born November 30 1719. Also the name of George III's second daughter, born November 8 1768.

Caroline — George II's Queen, born March 11 1683. Also George IV's estranged wife, born May 17 1768.

Louisa	Youngest daughter of George II, born December 7 1724.
Sophia	George I's mother, grand daughter of James I, through whom the British crown passed to the House of Hanover, born October 14 1630. Also Sophia Dorothea, the divorced wife of George I, born September 15 1666.

Male

Augustus	Sixth son of George III, born January 27 1773, later the Duke of Sussex.
Christian	Brother of George I, born September 19 1671.
Frederick	Son of George II, later Prince of Wales, born February 1 1707.
Maximillian	Brother of George I, born December 23 1666. His twin brother was stillborn.

VICTORIAN

Female

Alexandrina	First name of Queen Victoria, born May 24 1819.
Helena	Victoria's third daughter and fifth child, born May 25 1846.

Maud	Third and youngest daughter of Edward VII, born November 26 1869.
Victoria	The Queen who insisted all female descendants bear her name (see Alexandrina).

Male

Albert	Victoria's beloved, born August 26 1819.
Leopold	King of Belgians, uncle to both Victoria and Albert, also Princess Charlotte of Wales' widower, born December 16 1790.

Windsor

Female

Alice	Prince Philip's mother, born February 25 1885.

Male

Louis	Lord Mountbatten, Prince Philip's uncle, born June 25 1900.

Did You Know?

First Royal use of the name Mary in the British Isles was recorded in Scotland at the end of the eleventh century. This Mary was the youngest daughter of Scottish King Malcolm III.

—

A Bit of a Mouthful

Royalty tend to have more names than most. This is a relatively recent phenomenon. Until the seventeenth century, English and Scots' Princes and Princesses were given only one name. William I was just William, Robert the Bruce was the singular Robert, Elizabeth I plain Elizabeth. This started to change when the doubled-barrelled French Princess, Henrietta Maria, married the future Charles I in 1625. Two hundred and fifty years on and Victorian Royalty was taking 'name-trains' to extremes, bestowing on their offspring up to eight Christian names. Victoria decreed that all her female descendants take her name and all males that of her beloved Albert. Here are some of our favourite name combinations to be found amongst Victoria's extended family. . .

Victoria Mary Augusta Louise Olga Pauline Claudine Agnes. Eight names for the Victorian Princess, born May 26 1867, a first cousin once removed of Queen Victoria, who became Queen Mary when she married the future George V. Named for, amongst others, Queen Victoria; her mother (Mary); God mother (Augusta) and paternal grandmother (Claudine), she was known as 'May' after the month of her birth.

Sophia Dorothea Ulrica Alice. Daughter of Victoria's eldest child, Vicky, Empress of Prussia, Sophia was born June 14 1870 – 31 years before her grandmother's death – yet the name 'Victoria' does not figure in the line-up. Victoria the Queen cannot have been amused. Apart from 'Alice', each of these names belonged to previous Prussian Princesses.

Edward Albert Christian George Andrew Patrick David. Seven names for the boy born to be Edward VIII on June 24 1894. He was named Edward after Eddy, his father's dead brother (although Eddy had actually been christened Albert Victor rather than Edward). Second name Albert was after his great grand father; Christian after his godfather, the King of Denmark; and George, Andrew, Patrick and David - representing the patron saints of England, Scotland, Ireland and Wales respectively. He was known to friends and family simply as 'David'.

Victoria Alexandra Alice Mary. The only daughter of George V and Queen Mary, born April 25 1897, was named after her paternal great grandmother, her paternal grandmother, her great aunt and her maternal grandmother. It was by this last name that she was known.

Louis Francis Albert Victor Nicholas George. Six names for this great grandson of Queen Victoria, the uncle of the Duke of Edinburgh, born on June 25 1900. Note his names include both Albert and Victor, the masculine version of Victoria. The Queen herself was one of his godmothers.

Bertil Gustavus Oscar Charles Eugene. Another great grandson of Queen Victoria, he was the son of her grand daughter Princess Margaret of Connaught, who became Queen of Sweden. Born February 28 1912, some 11 years after Victoria's death, the name 'Albert' is missing. In fact, all baby Bertil's names reflected his Swedish rather than his British heritage.

Philippos. A simple, singular Greek name for this great, great grandson of Victoria who was born on a kitchen table in Corfu on June 10 1920. It was easily anglicized to Philip when he married into the British Royal Family and became the Duke of Edinburgh.

Margaret Rose. We're with George V on this one. Margaret Rose is far more fabulous, 1930s glamour than plain old Anne. But when, as an adult, this great great grand daughter of Victoria's (born August 21 1930) dropped the 'Rose', her name lost some of it's appeal. Some might say the Princess did, too.

> *Did You Know?*
> ___
>
> Prince Charles indirectly chose his niece
> Zara's name. Having read that Zara means
> 'radiance' in Arabic, he mentioned it to his
> sister, Anne, who loved it. Zara's middle
> names are the more traditional 'Anne' and
> 'Elizabeth'.

—

'NEVER AGAIN' NAMES

Call it superstition-of-the-sovereign kind but for all
the Marys, Elizabeths, Georges and Williams, there
are some names within the British Royal Family
which, however easy on the ear, have sad, mad or bad
connotations – or a combination of all three - and have
therefore been out of favour for years or even centuries.
There was controversy in 1948 when the infant son
of the then Princess Elizabeth and Prince Philip was
named 'Charles'. Now there was a 'bad-luck' name
if ever there was one. The baby boy's ancestor, King
Charles I, had been beheaded by his own countrymen
in 1649, while Charles II had a dubious, womanizing
reputation, lost two wars against the Dutch and died
without legitimate issue. Unbelievably there are still

some who believe that Charles should take his third name, 'Arthur', when he becomes King. While this name-change is highly unlikely, it will be interesting to see if, and when, the following names ever make a Royal come-back. . .

Charlotte. An extremely popular Royal name in Georgian Britain but, like so many previous favourites, the reason for its demise lies in tragedy. Charlotte Princess of Wales, the only child of George IV and Caroline of Brunswick, was heir to the throne and the nation's darling when she gave birth to a stillborn son on the evening of November 5 1817. Charlotte breathed her last the next morning. National grief was such that all shops, law courts, docks and the Royal Exchange closed their doors for two weeks. The name has been shunned in Royal circles - until now, perhaps. It is the middle name of Her Royal Hotness P-Middy, aka Catherine's younger sister, Pippa.

James. The name of Prince William's young cousin, James Wessex, aka Viscount Seven, the son of Edward and Sophie, but it is unlikely to be bestowed on a Royal baby close-to-the-throne due to its unhappy Stuart connections. The last British King named James – James II – was deposed in 1688 by his daughter and son-in-law (the future Mary II and William III) for being Catholic, pro French, and regarding himself as an absolute monarch. 'James' also has more recent unhappy 'Royal' family associations – think James Hewitt, the 'love-rat' lover of the late Diana. However James is also a Middleton name - Kate's brother answers to it.

Jane. The name of Henry VIII's third Queen, Jane Seymour, and also that of the Nine Day Queen, Lady Jane Grey, 'Jane' has not been bestowed on a British Royal since the sixteenth century, maybe because both 'Janes' died tragic deaths. Jane Seymour expired of puerperal or childbirth fever on October 24 1537 – 12 days after the birth of her infant son, the future Edward VI. Lady Jane Grey was executed by her cousin Queen Mary I (Bloody Mary) on February 12 1554 for being a pretender to the English throne.

NEVER AGAIN JANE

John. Possibly the unluckiest Royal name of all, King John (1199-1216) was widely, if unjustifiably, regarded as a useless King with the result that 'John', although for centuries one of the most popular names in Britain, never became a popular Royal name. King Robert III of Scotland (1390-1406) was baptized as John but sought a dispensation to change his name to Robert - a former King John of Scotland (John Balliol) having shamed his nation by abdicating to the English a century earlier. Prince Alexander John, the infant son of Edward VII and Alexandra, died the day after his birth on April 6 1871. Prince John, the fifth son of George V and Queen Mary, born July 12 1905, was epileptic and forced to live apart from his family until his death in 1919. Princess Diana wished 'John' (her father's name) to be one of the names bestowed on Prince William but this was discouraged due to its unlucky connotations. 'John' could be regarded as an unlucky Spencer name, too. Diana's brother who was called John died within 10 hours of his birth on January 12 1960.

Richard. He lived in the late 1400s but King Richard III is one of the most maligned monarchs in history, and his tyrannical, hunch-backed reputation has been kept alive by the Shakespeare play. It's debatable that he was as wicked as portrayed. Could be that Henry VII, rather than Richard, was responsible for the death of the little Princes in the Tower. But give a King a bad name and all that. . . His own name has been out of favour with heirs to the throne since his death at the Battle of Bosworth on August 22 1485.

Stephen. Why has there been no Prince or King named Stephen in Britain since the reign of the one-and-only Stephen I in the middle of the twelfth century? Could it be because his 19 year reign was marked by a fierce civil war with his cousin, rival, and rightful heir to the throne, Matilda, who was passed over because of her sex? When Stephen died in October 1154, Matilda had her revenge - it was her son Henry (Henry II) who succeeded to the throne rather than his son, William.

Did You Know?

The Queen's eldest grandson answers to the name of 'Peter' but no King Peter has ever sat on the British throne. Fortunate perhaps when you consider the unlucky non-British monarchs who have borne the name. In 1831 Peter or Pedro I of Brazil abdicated, while in 1889 his son and successor Pedro II was forced to flee to Europe after the republican revolution. Pedro the Cruel of Castile was killed by his brother in 1369, Russian Emperor, Peter II, ruled for just three years and died of smallpox in 1730 aged just 15, and in 1762 Peter III was dethroned and tortured on the orders of his wife, Catherine the Great.

'Never' Names - Period

There will never be a Prince Fin, Kai, or Cruz. Nor a Princess Willow, Suri, Shiloh or Apple. But there are also some names, including those with Cambridge family connections, which are highly unlikely to make it onto a Royal birth certificate. . .

Carole. The 1950s-tastic name of Catherine's highly fragrant mother is perhaps a little too, dare-we-say, lower middle class to make it onto a Cambridge Princess' birth certificate – even if the masculine version was favoured by the Kings of Romania. Caroline then? Possibly. It sounds aristocratic and already has something of a blue-blooded heritage in the form of George II's Queen. Then again as Carole (the woman not the name) is much-loved by her daughter and son-in-law, and is also said to be a favourite of the Queen's, maybe Carole (the name not the woman) will become Royalized after all.

Dorothy and **Edith**. While 'Elizabeth', the name of Prince William's paternal grandmother (and maybe that of 'Frances' his maternal grandmother, too) may well be bestowed on a little Cambridge Princess, it's unlikely that the names of Catherine's grandmothers,

Dorothy and Edith, will figure in the line-up. Yet both names have a Royal pedigree. There was a fifteenth century Queen of Bosnia called Dorothy, while Edith of Wessex was the Queen Consort of Edward the Confessor.

'Oliver'. There has never been a Prince Oliver – and there never will be. To give a close-to-the-throne Royal baby the same name as Oliver Cromwell, the man who, in the mid 1600s, overthrew the English monarchy, beheaded the King and temporarily turned England into a republic, would be self-treason.

king Oliver Cromwell

'Ron' and **'Gary'**. Prince Ron after Kate's maternal grand dad? Prince Gary after her scandal-prone uncle? No chance! Her paternal grandfather was named Peter and given that name's unfortunate Royal pedigree, that's not very likely, either.

'**Wallis**'. It is many years since the Duchess of Windsor died but her memory still looms large over the Royal house she married into. Even if Wallis was secretly Catherine's favourite name (highly unlikely but you never know), she'd do well to keep it under her tiara.

Did You Know?

Diana originally wanted William to be called Oliver but Prince Charles decided it had to be a more conventional name given the unfortunate historical connotations of Oliver.

PET NAMES

Coochy-coo! Royals are like the rest of us when it comes to their babies – they can't help but give their little darlings affectionate diminutives. Here's a whole menagerie of pet names that were bestowed on certain Royal personages when they were wee.

'Baby'. Princess Beatrice, born April 14 1857, was Victoria and Albert's ninth and final child, and therefore undeniably their baby – hence the pet name. But Victoria was still calling Bea 'Baby' when she was a married woman with babies of her own.

'Dickie'. Richard wasn't one of Louis Mountbatten's six names so how come he was known as Dickie? It's thanks to Tsar Nicholas II who visited Britain in 1909. Until this point little Prince Louis was known as Nicky (the derivative of his fifth name Nicholas) but then so was the Tsar. To avoid confusion, Tsar Nicky started calling little Nicky, 'Dickie'. It stuck and from then on, little Nicky was forever known as Dickie!

'Lilibet'. Elizabeth II coined her own nickname when, as a toddler, she was unable to pronounce Elizabeth. She's been called Lilibet by her family ever since.

'**The Bambino**'. Queen Mary's pet name for Elizabeth II when a baby.

'**Pussy**'. The pet name given to Victoria and Albert's eldest child, Vicky, born November 21 1840. Given its modern slang meaning, it's highly doubtful a Princess would answer to it today,

prince Albert &
his two
pussies

'**Sunny**'. The childhood nickname of Princess Alexandra of Hesse (born June 6 1872), the future wife of Tsar Nicholas II of Russia, and a grand daughter of Queen Victoria by her daughter, Princess Alice.

Unfortunately, once she'd reached adulthood Sunny wasn't sunny at all, and had become depressed and reclusive. But maybe she had reason. Her only son was a haemophiliac, she hated her mother-in-law and adopted country, plus she and her family were held captive after the revolution of 1917 and eventually executed.

'Wombat', 'Willy Wombat' and **'His Royal Naughtiness'**. Diana's pet names for her first-born son.

Did You Know?

If Queen Victoria had had her way, her great-granddaughter, Mary, daughter of the future George V and Queen Mary, would have been christened 'Diamond', because she was born during the Queen's Diamond Jubilee year (1897). Mary's parents refused, and Her Majesty had to be satisfied with calling Mary *'my little Diamond Jubilee baby'.*

ROYAL CHRISTENINGS

These days, christenings of the Regal kind tend to be family affairs but time was when they were sumptuous state occasions, designed to show off not just the new Royal baby but the riches, pomp and ceremony of the Court.

Henry VI's only son, **Edward of Westminster**, was christened in Westminster Abbey in October 1453. The font was arranged in russet cloth of gold and surrounded by a blaze of tapers. The christening mantle (robe) cost £500 (hundreds of thousands of pounds today) and was a rich embroidery of pearls and precious stones, lined with fine white linen to insure the brocade and gems didn't come into contact with the baby's delicate skin. Unfortunately Henry himself was unaware of such christening grandeur as he was in a state of mental collapse.

Arthur, Prince of Wales. The first-born son of Henry VII and Elizabeth of York arrived a month prematurely so arrangements for his lavish christening were brought forward. The baptism took place at Winchester Cathedral on September 24 1486 - the baby having been born in the town four days earlier as Henry VII had wished, believing Winchester to be the site of King Arthur's Camelot. Following the baptism, the christening party proceeded to the shrine of St Swithun, the cathedral's saint, where hymns were sung and *'spices and hypocras, with other sweet wines (in) great plenty'* enjoyed.

Edward VI. Christened at the chapel at Hampton Court on October 15 1537 in a lavish midnight ceremony in front of 400 people, this was the first christening of a prince in England for more than a quarter of a century, and every care was taken to make the event as elaborate and impressive as possible. The three-day-old Prince was carried under a canopy wearing a richly decorated *'chrisom cloth'*, his wet-nurse and midwife walked alongside the bearers of the train, and torchbearers surrounded the canopy. After the Prince had been baptized by the Archbishop of Canterbury, spice, hippocras, bread and sweet wine were served and then the torch-lit procession made its way out of the Chapel back to the Queen's apartments. Christening gifts included a gold cup from the Lady Mary (the prince's half sister and also his godmother), three bowls and two pots of silver and gilt from the Archbishop, and two flagons and two pots of silver and gilt from the Duke of Suffolk.

James I and VI of Scotland. His three-day Catholic christening took part at Stirling Castle in December 1566 when he was six-months-old. His mother, Mary Queen of Scots, refused to let the Archbishop of St Andrews, whom she referred to as '*a pocky priest*', spit in the child's mouth, as was then the custom. The entertainment culminated in a banquet in the Great Hall. The guests sat at a round table, in imitation of King Arthur and his knights, and the food was brought in on a mobile stage drawn by satyrs and nymphs. The English guests were offended because they were depicted as satyrs with tails. A child dressed as an angel was lowered in a giant globe from the ceiling and gave a recitation. The banquet ended with a great fireworks display – the first ever witnessed in Scotland.

Charles II. For the baptism of the future Charles II at the Chapel Royal on June 27 1630, the Lord Mayor of London presented him with a silver font. The four-week-old baby's attendants were awarded the following gifts – a chain of rubies for the wet-nurse, silver plate for the dry-nurse, a selection of silver spoons, cups and salt cellars for the six official cradle rockers. The baby Prince himself received the gift of a jewel from an uncle.

George IV. The baptism of the month-old, first-born son and heir of King George III in September 1762 was an occasion for as much splendour as the proud new father could muster. A new gilded mahogany state bed *'of superlative magnificence'* - embellished and ornamented with carvings, white ostrich plumes, gold lace-trimmed crimson velvet valances and curtains, and five mattresses - was built for Queen Charlotte to lounge upon during the ceremony. The regal new mother's head rested against a *'white satin pillow bordered with flowers worked in gold and spangles'.*

Princess Victoria. The first child of Queen Victoria and Prince Albert was christened on their first wedding anniversary, February 10 1841, wearing a specially commissioned gown, made from the same fabrics as her mother's wedding dress – Spitalfields silk satin and Honiton lace. The baby *'looked very dear in a white*

Honiton point lace robe and mantle, over white satin,' wrote the Queen. This became the most famous Royal christening gown. After this first wearing, it was worn by more than 60 Royal babies before it was 'retired' due to its deteriorating condition. Queen Elizabeth II commissioned a replica from her dresser, Angela Kelly, as a replacement. The last royal baby to wear the original gown was Lady Louise Windsor, daughter of the Earl and Countess of Wessex in 2004, while her younger brother, Viscount Severn was the first to wear the new gown in 2008. It has since been worn by Savannah and Isla, the daughters of Peter and Autumn Phillips, Elizabeth II's first two great grandchildren, at their christenings. The Lily Font, designed by Prince Albert, was first used at this baptism of baby Vicky – Queen Victoria objected to an earlier font because the illegitimate children of one of her predecessors had been christened in it!

Prince Albert Edward. For his christening in January 1842 at St George's Chapel, Windsor, his mama, Queen Victoria, spent thousands of pounds creating an event of *'unprecedented grandeur'*. Two royal baptismal fonts were used – the 1630 font, re-gilt and ornamented for the occasion, was used in conjunction with the new Lily Font. The christening celebrations included a banquet, fireworks and other entertainments and a christening cake '*on a scale of magnitude and magnificence quite unrivalled, (it) stands on a silver plateau about 30 inches in diameter, and is, with its figured ornaments, upwards of 4 feet high. Without its ornaments it would appear like a Coliseum of sugar*'. The Queen wore state jewels, the women wore evening dresses and tiaras, and the men wore uniforms and decorations.

Prince Charles. Three main cakes were made for Prince Charles' christening held in the Music Room of Buckingham Palace in December 1948 when he was little over a month old. All were on display in the White Drawing Room where a family reception was held after the ceremony. The principal cake was – as tradition dictated - the redecorated top tier of his parents' wedding cake. It featured intricate lace work done in icing and was topped with a silver cradle in which a baby doll, dressed in a christening gown by the Royal School of Art Needlework, slept. Students from the National Bakery School concocted the second confection - a sturdy, square-shaped cake topped with a coronet. The third cake was comprised of two tiers and was decorated with small silver charms and other silver ornaments made by war-disabled ex-service silversmiths. Lastly, a smaller cake, made for a *'private celebration'*, was baked by Mrs. Barnes, the cook at Prince Charles' parents' rented country house, Windlesham Moor in Berkshire. Mrs. Barnes *'was obliged to limit the amount of sugar in the cake'* due to war-time rations that were still in effect. Cakes apart, Queen Mary was thrilled with her great grandson. She wrote in her diary on the day of the christening: *'I gave the baby a silver gilt cup & cover which George III had given to a godson in 1780'*, and added proudly *'I gave a present from my great grandfather, to my great grandson 168 years later.'*

Did You Know?

At Princess Diana's christening at the Church of Mary Magdelene at Sandringham, Norfolk, in August 1961, her future husband Prince Charles, then aged 12, was one of the guests.

Tales from the Front

It's the same in every family. A gathering of the clans at a wedding, funeral or christening inevitably causes a certain amount of drama. It's the latter occasion we're concerned with here, of course, and being rather a theatrical bunch, Royals throughout history have regularly turned on the histrionics when a new member has been officially named.

Holy crap! According to William of Malmesbury, as a small child in the 970s, King Ethelred the Unready defecated in the baptismal font. This led Saint Dunstan to prophesy that the English monarchy would be overthrown during Ethelred's reign. Indeed it was - the Danes invaded in 980, two years after Ethelred had ascended the throne.

For the christening of the three-day-old Elizabeth I on September 10 1533, her father Henry VIII asked his wronged, first wife Catherine of Aragon for the *'very rich triumphal cloth'* she had brought with her from Spain for *'to wrap up her children with at baptism'*, and in which their only daughter Mary had been baptized 17 years earlier. Not surprisingly, Catherine refused. The christening itself was full of pomp and ceremony, the French Ambassador reporting that '*the whole occasion was so perfect that nothing was lacking*'. Actually it was – Henry had cancelled the planned celebratory joust because the little Princess wasn't a Prince. Elizabeth, with no '*triumphal*' shawl to wear, was dressed in a royal mantle of purple velvet with a long train furred with ermine.

The christening in November 1717 of the fifth child of the future George II and his Queen, Caroline, was the scene of a feud between the couple and George's father, King George I. They wanted to choose the baby's godparents but the King insisted he should. A bitter fall-out resulted. George and Caroline were put under house arrest, and subsequently banished from their home at St James's Palace. The King also took over the guardianship of his grandchildren and only allowed their parents to visit when he gave permission. As for the baby Prince who was named George William? He died aged just four months.

The mother of Queen Victoria was reduced to tears at the christening of her baby daughter at Kensington Palace in June 1819 due to the behaviour of her brother-in-law, the Prince Regent. He only told the baby's parents the date of the christening at the very last minute, dictated what the baby's name should be – Alexandrina Victoria, and insisted that only he, out of the baby's godparents, be present. He also refused to speak to the baby's father who was also his brother, and refused to attend the post-christening dinner afterwards.

At the christening of Queen Victoria's second daughter, Princess Alice, in 1843, the Queen's uncle, the King of Hanover, arrived late for the ceremony, behaved rudely, *'never (spoke) a kind word'*, and made a public fuss about the dispute with his niece over the ownership of the late Queen Charlotte's jewels.

Victoria couldn't resist having a bit of a bitch about the christening of a grandson, Prince Alfred, at Buckingham Palace on November 23 1874 when the baby prince was five-weeks-old. *'The christening I thought a flat, dull affair,'* she wrote to her daughter, Princess Louise. *'The room was so badly arranged and might have been prettily so - and tho' very large - people did not see as well as they might have done.'*

At the baptism of the future George VI in early 1896, the future Edward VIII, then aged a year-and-a-half, behaved impeccably until his baby brother started to yell. Edward decided to yell even louder and was promptly removed.

A few minutes before the baptism of Lord Louis Mountbatten on July 17 1900 at Frogmore House on the Windsor Castle estate, the month-old-baby accidentally knocked off the spectacles of his great grandmother, who also happened to be his godmother, Queen Victoria. It's not known if she was amused - or not - but she certainly managed to keep her cool on an extremely hot summer's day. She ordered that a bucket of ice should be placed under her chair.

Before his christening in Spring 1960, two-month old Prince Andrew pee'ed on his new nanny! *'He christened me before we went,'* she wrote in her journal. *'I had him on his pot, not thinking, of course. He mis-aimed and I went to the Royal christening with a damp skirt!!'*

Prince William's christening on August 4 1982 wasn't a particularly happy occasion for his mother, Diana, who recalled. *'I was treated like nobody else's business. Nobody asked me if it was suitable for William – 11 o'clock couldn't have been worse. Endless pictures of the Queen, the Queen Mother, Charles and William. I was excluded that day. I wasn't very well and I just blubbed my eyes out. William started crying, too. Well, he just sensed that I wasn't exactly hunky dory.'*

At Prince Harry's christening in St George's Chapel, Windsor Castle on December 21 1984, his father, Prince Charles, allegedly moaned that he had wanted his second child to be a girl. Diana's mother, Frances Shand Kydd, reportedly gave him a mouthful, telling him he should be grateful for a healthy child whatever the sex.

Did You Know?

———

The future Queen Elizabeth II apparently cried so much at her christening that '*her nurse dosed her with dill water*', an old-fashioned remedy, much to the amusement of her uncle, the Prince of Wales, later Edward VIII.

—

ROYAL GODPARENTS

The custom of choosing a godparent for a baptism originated in Roman times, the original word for godparent being 'patronus', meaning 'protector'. In the Royal Family, godparents are known as 'sponsors' and it is their duty to give advice (when asked) on the spiritual life of the Royal child. This must be a rather daunting responsibility when said child is close to the Crown. The Royals have always kept it 'in the family' when it comes to choosing godparents – uncles, aunts, brothers, sisters, cousins and, until relatively recently, even grandparents figure heavily. The closer-to-the -throne the baby, the more blue-blooded, it seems, are the sponsors but this still doesn't explain why Royal babies have so many godparents– far more than the usual three. Maybe it's just because they can!

One of Tudor **Prince Arthur's** godfathers was over three hours late for his christening. John de Vere, the 13th Earl of Oxford, was still travelling to Winchester from his home in Lavenham, Suffolk and didn't make it to the Cathedral on time for the christening in September 1485.

Louis XII of France was godfather to Prince Henry, Duke of Cornwall, the baby son of Henry VIII and Catherine of Aragon who lived for only seven weeks after his birth on January 1 1511. The French King wrote to them after the January 5 baptism – which he didn't attend – saying he would send a chain of 200 crowns to the Prince's nurse, and insisted that she be told that the King of France was praying her to nurse well his godson. Sadly this wasn't enough to save the baby.

Charles II was godfather to Charles Fitzroy, one of his children by mistress Barbara Palmer, declaring '*he is my son*' at the baby's christening in 1662. While in 1874 the future Edward VII was godfather to George Cornwallis-West, thought to be his illegitimate son by one of his many mistresses, Patsy Cornwallis-West.

Princess Anne is not godmother to any of her

brothers' children even though Charles is godfather to her son, Peter Phillips, and Prince Andrew is Zara's godfather.

As a '*disappointing*' third daughter, **Princess Diana** was not blessed with Royal godparents – unlike her siblings. Eldest sister Sarah had Queen Elizabeth, the Queen Mother as a godmother, elder sister Jane had the Duke of Kent as a godfather, while younger brother Charles is a godson of Elizabeth II. Diana's godparents were non Royal, although one of her godmothers is thought to have been the wife of a Colonel!

Queen Victoria was godmother to two of her grandchildren, including the grandson whose '*dull*' christening she complained about, and also four of her great grandchildren, including the future Edward VIII and George VI.

Edward VIII is the British Royal with the most godparents. He had 12 - two Kings, three Queens, two Princes, one Princess, one Duchess, two Dukes and one Grand Duke.

One of the **Prince Michael of Kent's** godfathers was American President Franklin D Roosevelt, although he was unable to attend the christening at Windsor on August 4 1942, and the baby's father, The Duke of Kent, stood proxy. 'Franklin' is also one of Prince Michael's middle names - a fitting tribute for a baby born on the fourth of July.

Just call me franklin D

Crown Prince Felipe of Spain was baptized on February 8, 1968 and his godmother was his great-grandmother, 80-year-old Queen Victoria Eugenia of Spain, a grand daughter of Queen Victoria. She died the year later.

Did You Know?

Baby Prince and Princesses from Catholic countries have only one or two godparents - as laid down by Canon Law.

VI

WRONG SIDE
OF THE
ROYAL BLANKET

———

'A King is supposed to be the father of his people and Charles certainly was the father to many of them'

The Duke of Buckingham on King Charles II's 'habit' of siring illegitimate children.

Babies born out of wedlock used to be an occupational hazard for Royalty. Neither frowned upon nor officially celebrated, it was simply something that happened. In Ancient Rome, Emperors were more concerned with the continuity of family name than bloodline. If a man recognized a child as his own, it was accepted by law. In Anglo-Saxon times, all descendants – legitimate and illegitimate - of Kings were known as 'aelthings'. When the office of King became vacant, a successor would be chosen from amongst them. By medieval times, despite the fact that the illegitimate William Duke of Nomandy, had become King of England in 1066, 'bastard' sons were not regarded as rightful heirs. Monarchs did, however, regularly employ 'natural children' in their service, making their sons governors of provinces and generals in the army - loyalty to the Crown assured by blood. Meanwhile a good marriage was assured for a Monarch's natural daughter. For a King's mistress, giving him children could be a canny career move. But while some Royal baby-mothers were provided for and did indeed benefit from their status as the mother of a Monarch's child, others were unceremoniously dumped and left penniless. For Royal Princesses who found themselves pregnant but unmarried there was no happy ending. Their babies would be adopted and rarely heard of again. Not for them the extended familial atmosphere, prestige and, on occasions, stark nepotism enjoyed by so many illegitimate offspring of a Prince or King.

Did You Know?

If Princess Grace of Monaco were still alive, she'd have three 'natural' grandchildren as well as her six 'born-in-wedlock' ones. Her son Prince Albert II has two known 'love' children – a daughter Jazmin Grace Grimaldi (born March 4 1992) by Tamara Rotolo, and a son Alexandre Coste (born August 24 2003) by Nicole Coste. Grace's daughter Stephanie has one 'love' child in addition to her two legitimate ones. Camille Kelly Marie Gottlieb was born July 15 1998 and although her father is not identified on her birth certificate, he is thought to be former Palace guard, Jean-Raymond Gottleib.

Who's The Daddy?

Since 1066, at least 150 children have been fathered, out of wedlock, by English and Scottish Kings. Indeed for hundreds of years it was practically a badge of honour and any King or Prince worth his orb and sceptre had at least one 'natural' child to his name. Ditto the male Monarchs throughout Europe. It was the rule rather than the exception. But then Victoria came to the British throne in 1837 and quickly reversed this particular Royal trend. *'Ghosts best forgotten'* is how she referred to her many illegitimate cousins. However the spectre of illegitimacy began to haunt the Monarchy once more when her licentious son and heir, the future Edward VII, made infidelity his life's work. He never publicly acknowledged fathering any children out of wedlock – probably because he knew how badly his mother, and also his wife Alexandra would have taken it – but it's generally thought that he did. But more of that later. . . Here, we are concerned with which British King or Prince sired the most demi-royals and is therefore the daddy of them all!

25

Henry I. This dark-haired, muscular, fourth son of William the Conqueror who ruled between 1100 and 1135 begat approximately 25 children out of wedlock. The mothers included his mistresses Sybilla Fitzherbert, a widow named Ansfrida, a Welsh Princess and a Duke's daughter from Cumberland. Many of the children were born by unknown women. Ironically only one of his four legitimate children with his long-suffering wife Matilda, a Scottish princess, survived into adulthood – a daughter also called Matilda.

16

Charles II. A total of eight women gave birth to Charles II's 16 illegitimate children, including Orange girl Nell Gwyn (two) and formidable beauty Barbara Castlemaine (six). Dark of hair, swarthy of skin and full of lips, the easy-going Charles willingly bestowed titles on his 'natural' offspring - although Nell, being a *'common whore'*, had to manipulate the situation in order to get her boys ennobled. On a visit from Charles when their elder boy, also called Charles, was six-years-old, Nell told him to, *'Come here, you little bastard, and say hello to your father.'* When the King protested at her words, she replied, *'Your Majesty has given me no other name by which to call him.'* Little Charles was duly created the Duke of St Albans and his younger brother James, Lord Beauclerk.

12

Henry II. Had three children by a woman called Ikenai who was known as a *'common prostitute'*, including Geoffrey whom Henry later made Archbishop of York. Four children were born to Alice, the daughter of Louis VII of France, who at the time had been betrothed to Henry's legitimate son, Richard (later the Lionheart) – sadly all died young. One son was born to Nesta, the wife of a Knight; another child to a lady named Alice de Porhoet; and there were three further children, including an Abbess of Barking and a Bishop of Lincoln, by women unknown.

King John. Short and stocky he may have been but auburn-haired King John who ruled between 1199 and 1216 sowed his Royal seed far and wide – just like his father. In addition to the five legitimate children he had with his Queen, Isabella, there were a dozen illegitimate ones – many of whom were known as FitzRoy (from the Norman 'son of the king') or FitzJohn ('son of John'). These children were borne to several different women.

11

William IV. None of his legitimate children survived but he had enough illegitimate ones for a soccer team. His first-born, also named William, was the child of Caroline von Linsingen who alleged the future King had secretly married her in 1784/5, around the time of her son's birth. There was never any proof to support her claim and sadly little William drowned in 1807. The other 10 children (five boys and five girls known collectively as the FitzClarences) were borne to his long-term mistress, actress Dorothea Jordan. These were the '*Ghosts*' referred to by Queen Victoria.

9

James V of Scotland. While he had only one living legitimate child, Mary Queen of Scots, he had more than enough illegitimate ones – seven boys and two girls. He fathered three of them before he was 20. The young King was said to have been encouraged in his amorous affairs by the Angus regime in order to distract him from politics. All nine children had different mothers with several of his sons, three of whom were called James, entering the church.

8

Robert II of Scotland. The 10 children from his first marriage were regarded by some as being not quite legitimate due to the fact that he and his wife, Elizabeth Mure, were lovers before they were married – although a Papal dispensation was obtained in 1347. But this apart, the grandson of Robert the Bruce fathered eight natural children – all boys. The mother of the eldest, John, is traditionally known as Moira Leitch but it's not known who were the mothers of his brothers, two of whom were also named John.

7

James II of England. Like his brother Charles II, James liked the ladies yet only two of his many mistresses are thought to have borne him children. From 1667-1674 Lady Arabella Churchill gave birth to two daughters and two sons. Catherine Sedley, her successor, gave birth to James daughter who lived to adulthood and married into the aristocracy, and also two sons who died in babyhood. *King Richard III of England* also had seven illegitimate children, all by mothers unknown, the eldest of whom is said to have been murdered in 1499.

6

Robert the Bruce. The famous fourteenth century Scottish King had five legitimate children from two marriages but a further six out of wedlock – the mothers of whom are all unknown. What *is* known is that he made his eldest illegitimate son, also called Robert, Lord of Liddesdale. *King Harold*, defeated by William I in 1066, also had six 'love' children – all by his mistress, Edith Swanneshals or Swan Neck.

5

King Stephen. Four 'natural' sons and one 'natural' daughter for the last Norman King. Three sons, including his beloved eldest, Gervaise, were by Dameta, a Normandy gentlewoman, while the identities of the mothers of his fourth son and singleton daughter are not known.

4

Edward IV. A notorious womanizer, it's surprising that this Yorkist King is only thought to have had four children out of wedlock - a boy named Edward who died in infancy in 1468 along with his mother Eleanor Talbot; a son and daughter by mistress Elizabeth Lucy, and a daughter, Grace, by a woman unknown. If, however, Edward was himself illegitimate as was suggested by his brother Richard III, then his nine 'legitimate' children by Queen Elizabeth Woodville were illegitimate, too.

3

Edward III. One son and two daughters by his mistress, Alice Perrers. Thought to have been illegitimate herself, Alice was lady-in-waiting to his Queen, Phillippa, and became his mistress when she was just 15 in 1363, six years before Phillippa's death. Edward was 51 at the time but it's said that Alice seduced him! The scandal was hushed up until heartbroken Phillippa died in 1369, at which point Edward lavished gifts on Alice, giving her land and even some of the late Queen's jewels, worth six million pounds in today's money. Alice and Edward's children all made 'good' marriages.

George I had three illegitimate daughters named, Anna Luise, Petronilla and Margaret by his extremely tall, skinny mistress, the Duchess of Kendal, who was nicknamed 'The Beanpole'.

2

King Richard I. He was rumored to be homosexual but 'The Lionheart' is thought to have had two illegitimate sons – Fulk by Joan de la Pol, and Philip who became Lord of Cognac by an unknown mother.

1

Edward II. Also thought to be gay, nonetheless Edward had an illegitimate son named Adam by an unknown mother, in addition to his four legitimate children with Isabella of France.

Henry VII also fathered one illegitimate child before he became King, Roland de Velville, who became Constable of Beaumaris Castle in Anglesey, Wales.

Henry VIII, Henry VII''s legitimate son, only ever acknowledged Henry Fitzroy, by mistress Bessie Blount, as his son. But it's believed he may also have fathered a daughter by Bessie, plus a second daughter and three further sons – including Henry Carey, the son of Mary Boleyn, who is said to have greatly resembled the King.

Did You Know?

The eighteenth century King Augustus II of Poland, known as 'Augustus the Strong', sired over 300 illegitimate children.

The Kings' Favourites

Illegitimate Royal children were generally the result of a love affair between a King or Prince and his mistress. The gene pool was, therefore, much larger than it was when first and second blue-blooded cousins married and reproduced. In the main, Royal bastards were better looking, healthier and more intelligent than their half brothers and sisters who had probably been conceived more out of duty than love. Being unaware of the scientific facts behind this, it was believed Royal bastards were more impressive because an act of love produced superior children than those created from a forced mating. Some illegitimate Royal children were actually preferred to their legal half-siblings. 'Natural' children completely relied on their Royal fathers' goodwill – without that they had nothing. In return for his generosity and patronage, such children would be loving and loyal. Some Kings also had favourites within their brood of illegitimate children. . .

Henry I and his first-born illegitimate son, *Robert Duke of Gloucester*. Known as 'Rufus', a Norman family name, King Henry became particularly close to Robert after the sinking of the 'White Ship' in which his sole surviving legitimate son, William, drowned

– as did two of his illegitimate children, Richard and Matilda Fitzroy. William had perished trying to save his half sister. As a result grieving King Henry made Robert, the Duke of Gloucester. Robert came to the aid of his half sister, the King's legitimate daughter who was also called Matilda, by becoming her chief military supporter during the civil war known as 'The Anarchy', in which she vied with Stephen of Blois for the throne of England.

Gervase de Blois was the illegitimate son of King Stephen and his mistress, Damette. His father appointed him Abbot of Westminster Abbey in the second half of 1138, despite the fact that Gervase was only in his teens – a case of nepotism if ever there was. But shortly after Stephen died in 1154 and King Henry II, son of Matilda, claimed the throne, Gervase was deposed.

Henry II and his bastard son *Geoffrey Plantagenet.* As Henry lay dying in 1179, it was Geoffrey who sat at his bedside. Richard and John, the King's surviving legitimate sons, had gone against their father and sided with the King of France. '*You alone have proved yourself my lawful and true son,*' the ailing Henry is reported to have said to Geoffrey. '*My other sons are really the bastards.*'

Adam FitzRoy was the illegitimate son of Edward II of England, born around 1305 – before Edward became King in 1308. The identity of his mother is not known. Adam is named as '*Ade filio domini Regis bastardo*' (*Adam, bastard son of the Lord King*) in Edward II's Wardrobe account of 1322 and he was awarded a total of thirteen pounds and twenty-two pence to buy himself '*equipment and other necessaries*' in order to take part in Edward's Scottish campaign that autumn. Sadly Adam died during the campaign and was buried at Tynemouth Priory on September 30 1322 - his father paid for a silk cloth with gold thread to be placed over his body. Unlike the legitimate son and heir, Edward, Prince of Wales, who along with his mother, Isabella of France, deposed King Edward II and had him murdered, Adam Fitzroy was always loyal to his father.

James, Duke of Monmouth. Born on April 9 1649, James was Charles II's second-born illegitimate son (his first, also named James born five years before to a lady named Marguerite de Carteret, became a Jesuit Priest). There were rumours that Charles and Lucy Waters, the future Duke's mother, had secretly married which would have made James the legitimate heir to the throne but although Charles recognized

James as his son, he did not name him as his heir. Learning that Lucy wasn't properly taking care of little James, said to be his father in miniature, Charles, who was still in exile in France, had James placed in the care of his own mother, the boy's grandmother, Queen Henrietta Maria. When he was 14, James was sent to Britain, proclaimed Duke of Monmouth and married to the wealthy Anne Scott, 4th Countess of Buccleuch. In 1672 Charles made his son Commander-in-Chief of the English Army and Captain-General in 1678, but after James was implicated in a plot to assassinate both Charles and his legitimate heir, James Duke of York, James Monmouth exiled himself to Holland. He hoped to accede peacefully to the English throne when

James Duke of Monmouth

his father died but the accession of James II put an end to these hopes. He attempted a rebellion against his uncle but was defeated and executed.

The French *King Henri IV* far favoured his illegitimate son, *Cesar Duc de Vendome,* over his legal son and heir, the Dauphin. '*See how good-natured this son is and how much he resembles me?*' Henri would boast. When, in 1606, a coach carrying the Royal Family, including Cesar, overturned in a river during a flash flood, Henry grabbed Cesar and ran to safety with the boy in his arms. The rest of the family was left to fend for themselves. All eight of Henri's bastards, by various mistresses, were raised alongside his six legitimate children – much to the dismay of Henri's Queen, Marie de Medici. The King insisted upon it. He visited his offspring regularly but found it difficult to remember all their names.

Anna Karolina Orzelska was a daughter of *Augustus the Strong* and a French wine merchant's daughter. She was her father's favourite child because she looked so much like him and, despite being poorly educated, she proved to be an excellent addition to court life. She lived scandalously, smoked, drank and had many love affairs – just like her dad. Anna Karolina also excelled at horse riding, dancing and hunting, and became the mistress of Frederick Wilhelm I of Prussia.

George FitzClarence, first Earl of Munster. The eldest of the future William IV's 10 illegitimate children with his long-term mistress, actress Mrs Jordan, the Duke proclaimed the baby to be *'very fine and perfect'*. 'Silly Billy', as the Duke was known, doted on all his natural children but George was his favourite. Indeed in 1830, when the Duke, aged 65, finally succeeded to the throne, he insisted that George, *'Our dearly beloved natural son'*, carry the crown at his coronation.

Did You Know?

Legend has it that Matilda of Flanders, the wife of William the Conqueror, initially refused to marry the future King while still Duke of Normandy, because he was illegitimate. The story goes that he sought her out and either pulled her off her horse, or pulled her out of her bed by her long braids. She then agreed to marry him to avoid a scandal.

Secret Sirings

Not all Kings and Princes have been willing to go public about the 'natural' fruit of their loins. Rumours abound about certain secret Royal sirings, but are rumours all they are? Here's the evidence, you decide.

George III. The story goes that George fathered three children by Hannah Lightfoot, the Quakeress he is said to have secretly married when he was just 15. Hannah and her children seem to have mysteriously disappeared shortly before George's dynastic duty called and he married German Princess, Charlotte of Mecklenburg Strelitz, in 1761 when he was 22.

George IV. This George never officially recognized any illegitimate children but the fact that Elizabeth Crole, the mother of a certain George Seymour Crole (born August 23 1799), received a £500 annuity from the privy purse is proof enough. According to Elizabeth, young George was *'accustomed to consider himself as the natural son of the King'* and when George IV died in 1830, his son was left a capital sum of £30,000 (worth over £1,000,000 today) plus a cash payment of £10,000 (£300,000 today). Crole's uncle, William IV, and cousin, Queen Victoria, also made provision for him until his death in 1863.

Edward VII. Like his great uncle George, Edward never officially recognized any illegitimate children but given he was as notorious a womanizer as Charles II, it's safe to say there were many. Most of his mistresses were respectably married women and were therefore able to pass off any regally begotten children as their husbands' – George Cornwallis West, son of Patsy Cornwallis West (born November 14 1874), Alexandra James Fawcus, daughter of Mrs Willy James (born December 1896), and The Honourable Maynard Greville, son of the Countess of Warwick (born March 21 1898) may well have been Edward's children. It has also been suggested that Winston Churchill, son

Edward VII

of Jennie Lady Randolf Churchill (born November 30 1875) was the then Prince of Wales son! But most intriguing of all is the likelihood that Sonia Rosemary Keppel, daughter of the King's last mistress Alice Keppel (born May 24 1900) was Edward's child. Sonia was the maternal grandmother of Camilla, Duchess of Cornwall, making Edward VII her possible great grandfather and Prince Charles a second cousin once removed in addition to being her husband! Good Old Teddy, as he was popularly known, is also thought to have fathered children by, amongst others, the Duke of Newcastle's daughter, a French Duchess, an Italian Duchess, a Colonel's wife, and ladies from Northern Ireland and Lincolnshire. And he didn't stop there. There are rumours that he spread his seed – willy-nilly – around north Norfolk as he impregnated random servant and village girls close to his Sandringham home!

George V. There were rumours that before his marriage to Princess May of Teck in 1893, George V, when Duke of York, contracted an illegal marriage with a woman in Malta and fathered three illegitimate children. When a French magazine published the story, George sued for libel - the journalist who had written the story was convicted and imprisoned. A recent rumour also alleges that Sir Anthony Blunt (born September 26 1907), Surveyor of the Queen's Pictures who was exposed as a Soviet spy in 1979, was also an illegitimate son of George V.

Edward VIII. In spite of his wife, Wallis Simpson, quipping that he wasn't '*heir-conditioned*', the odds are that the future Duke of Windsor, known as David, fathered at least one illegitimate child, quite possibly more. Australian grazier Anthony Chisholm (born 1921) is said to have been David's son – the product of a one-afternoon-stand with a Sydney girl, named Molly Little, whom he met while touring Australia in 1920. Lord Louis Mountbatten had her smuggled aboard the HMS Renown for an afternoon of passion with the Prince. Nine months later, Tony was born and is said to have been the image of his alleged Royal father, although not quite so petite. He was raised by his mother and her husband, Roy Chisholm, but is rumoured to have visited his birth father in Paris. Tony died in 1987. The only child of David's mistress Thelma, Lady Furness, is also thought to have been fathered by him. Born on March 31 1929, William Anthony, or Tony as he was known, could well have been conceived during the Kenyan safari, which the then Prince of Wales and Thelma took in 1928. Tony was given the Furness name but his official 'father', Marmaduke, was said to be vile to the boy because he was David's son. Certainly Tony, who died in 1995, considered himself to be of Royal blood and was upset when the Duke himself didn't recognize it. Many sources attest that actor Timothy Ward Seely (born June 10 1935) is the DoW's son by married society beauty Vera Seely, an old friend of the Prince's and the younger sister of his one-time mistress Freda Dudley Ward. The story goes that the two had a brief encounter in September 1934, resulting in the birth of Timothy nine months later. Timothy himself has said that he does not wish to tarnish the memory of his mother who died in 1970 but admits he has a definite physical resemblance to the Prince, and also a *short temper and flashes of arrogance*.

George, Duke of Kent. Youngest son of George V, bisexual George, allegedly fathered two illegitimate children in addition to his three legitimate ones by wife, Princess Marina. Romantic novelist Barbara Cartland believed him to be the father of her daughter, Raine (born September 9 1929), who incidentally became the stepmother of Princess Diana. The Duke was also said to have fathered a son by the drug addicted American socialite Kiki Preston, known as *'the girl with the silver syringe'*. George's brother, the future Edward VIII, believed the boy to be Michael Temple Caulfield (born August 9 1926). the adopted son of American publisher Cass Canfield, who later became the first husband of Lee Radziwell, the sister of Jacqueline Kennedy Onassis.

Prince Philip. Rumours aplenty that the Duke of Edinburgh has an illegitimate issue. An Australian magazine stated he'd fathered 25 out-of-wedlock children until realizing it was, in fact, 25 godchildren he had. Then again, throughout history, Royalty have often stood as sponsors to their 'natural' offspring. . .

Prince Charles. There are stories that the present Prince of Wales fathered an illegitimate child with a young servant girl at Balmoral Castle when he was 18 years old in 1967. Nothing more is known. . .

Did You Know?

According to Richard III, his elder brother Edward IV was actually only a half brother – and a non-Regal one at that. Richard's argument was that during the time Edward was conceived – between July 14 and August 21 1441 in order to match his birth date of April 28 1442 – his 'father', the Duke of York, was on campaign at Pontoise in France, which was several days march from Rouen where his wife Cecily was quartered. Certainly Edward grew up to look nothing like his small, dark, spare 'father' or any of his brothers for that matter. He was 6 feet 4 inches tall – an exceptional height for his time and it was mooted that his real father was an archer called Blaybourne.

—

MYSTERIOUS MOTHERS

When Kings or Princes throughout history made their lovers and mistresses pregnant, there was no pay back, no disgrace, no scandal or shame brought upon the family. Not so the Queens and Princesses who found themselves in a similar position. Such Royal Ladies were hidden away like the dirty secret they were believed to be. Thankfully times have changed. When Princess Stephanie of Monaco fell pregnant with her third child, Camille, in 1997, she refused to name the father on the birth certificate and has remained silent on the subject - although he's thought to be former Palace guard, Jean Raymond Gottlieb. Camille, although omitted from the line of succession, was immedaitely accepted and welcomed into the House of Grimaldi. Meanwhile Stephanie, always a maverick, never lost the love and support of her family, These Royal Ladies who found themselves in the 'non-legit' family way weren't nearly so fortunate.

In August 1800, 22 year-old unmarried *Princess Sophia*, the fifth daughter of George III, was *'brought to bed'* and gave birth to a son. His father is thought to have been General Thomas Garth, one of George III's equerries. At 30 years Sophia's senior, small in stature and disfigured by a large purple birthmark over his forehead and around one eye, Garth was hardly was heart throb material. He was, however, one of the few men Sophia and her closely

princess
sophia

guarded unmarried sisters were allowed to meet. It appears that one night nine months before the birth in Weymouth, Garth had sneaked up to Sophia's room at the Queen's Lodge in Windsor – the King and Queen being away in London - and made her pregnant. Sophia's son was christened Thomas and left in Weymouth at the home of Major Herbert Taylor, the Private Secretary to the Duke of York. George III had been told that Sophia had gone to Weymouth because she was suffering from Dropsy – a form of fluid retention, which she probably had considering her condition! When she returned to court, minus the 'water retention', the increasingly unhinged King was told she'd been miraculously cured by eating roast beef. General Garth accepted paternity of young Thomas and he remained in favour at Court. It is thought Sophia was occasionally able to visit Thomas in secret. There was an alternative, far more alarming, story that arose after the scandal finally broke in 1829, inferring that the boy was, in fact, fathered by Sophia's brother, Ernest, Duke of Cumberland, who, it was mooted, had always seemed to have an unnatural interest in his little sister. Sophia was perhaps not the only daughter of George III who gave birth to a secret, illegitimate child. It has been mooted that in 1788, **Princess Elizabeth**, the third daughter of George and

Charlotte, went through a form of marriage with Royal page's son, George Ramus, and bore him a daughter, Eliza, who was raised by the Ramus family. In 1818 when she was 48, Elizabeth finally escaped from the claustrophobic bosom of her family and married an obscure German Royal. She had no further children.

Maria Sophia Queen of Naples. Exiled to Rome after her fanatically religious husband, Francis II, lost his crown, Maria Sophia fell in love with an officer of the Papal Guard, Armand de Lawayss, and became pregnant by him. She retreated to her parents' home in Germany where a family council decided that she must give birth in secret to prevent scandal. On November 24 1862, Maria Sophie gave birth to a daughter in a German convent. The child was immediately given to Lawayss' family and Maria Sophia made to promise that she would never see her baby again. Maria Sophie suffered from depression in later life, believed to be connected to giving her baby away.

Princess Thyra of Denmark, the little sister of the future Queen Alexandra of Great Britain, was just 18 when she secretly gave birth to a daughter on November 8 1871. The baby's father was a lieutenant of the cavalry, Vilhelm Frimann Marcher, with whom she'd fallen in love and had an affair. There was no question of them marrying – a Princess simply could not marry a commoner. When it was discovered that Thyra was pregnant, her brother, King George I of Greece, suggested that she travel to Athens and have the baby there, pretending she had jaundice and was travelling due to ill health. The child, named Maria, was immediately whisked away and adopted by a Danish couple called Jorgenson who changed her name to Kate. It's unlikely Thyra ever saw or heard of her again. Marcher committed suicide two months after his baby daughter was born, having been banned by Thyra's father from seeing either his Royal lover or his daughter. When Thyra married the Duke of Cumberland seven years later and became pregnant, it is said that, throughout the nine months, she constantly heard the cries of a baby. Kate Jorgenson lived a long life and died in 1964, aged 93. Thyra's maternal aunt, **Princess Marie Luise Charlotte of Denmark**, is also thought to have given birth to an illegitimate child in the 1830s when, as a teenager, she had a secret affair with a stable hand.

Duchesse Marie of Mecklenberg. As a young woman Marie became pregnant by a servant - a married man named Hecht who was responsible for turning off the gas-lights in the bedrooms of the Grand Ducal children.

Several of Marie's cousins, including the future King George V of the United Kingdom and German Emperor Wilhelm II, thought that Marie had been '*hypnotized*' by Hecht while Queen Victoria thought she had been drugged. Hecht was dismissed from service on the charge of stealing - his subsequent law-suit against the Grand Ducal family made details of the story public, causing a massive scandal in Germany. A daughter was born to Marie in 1898 and raised under the protection of Marie's grandmother, Grand Duchess Augusta of Mecklenburg-Strelitz, Queen Victoria's first cousin.

Princess Margaret. Yes, that's right, the late sister of the Queen of England is also present in this category. A Jersey-based accountant by the name of Robert Brown is so convinced he is the secret love child of the Princess and Group Captain Peter Townsend, he is willing to spend over £100,000 in lawyers' fees trying to prove it. Brown was born on January 5 1955 although his birth was not registered until February 2. His birth mother is named as society model Cynthia Joan Brown, now deceased. His father, Douglas, was posted to Kenya with the Army. Robert maintains that his parents treated him quite differently to his younger siblings and when his mother handed him his birth certificate when he was in his early 20s, he recalls that '*It struck me as* *odd at the time. On her part devoid of emotion, slightly embarrassed and her manner did not seem to invite discussion.*' Brown's theory is that the couple agreed to adopt him in order to prevent a Royal scandal, and he claims to remember an isolated meeting with a woman whom he believes to have been Princess Margaret when he was two-years-old. He admits it sounds absurd but says Princess Margaret's diary was virtually empty up to and surrounding the date of his birth, and very few photographs of her were taken at this time – quite a departure when the Princess had been the cover girl of her day. He also points to the fact that the Princess was mysteriously taken ill around the time of his birth and that an emergency Privy Council meeting was held on the actual day. Margaret was then sent on a trip to the Caribbean, created at very short notice. Brown recently renewed his legal battle to prove he is the illegitimate son of Princess Margaret. His previous high court appeal for disclosure of her will in 2006 and 2007 were dismissed by the court and labeled *'imaginary and baseless'* but he is now fighting under freedom of information laws for access to the documents. If he is successful in proving that he is indeed Margaret's son and therefore Queen Elizabeth II's nephew, Brown will become 16th in line to the throne and stands to inherit millions.

Did You Know?

There was no hiding away by Catherine the Great when she fell pregnant outside wedlock. The all-powerful eighteenth century Russian Empress famously had many lovers and three illegitimate children – Anna Petrovna born December 9 1757 (fathered by the future King Stanislaus II of Poland), Elizabeth Alexandrovna Alexeeva born in 1761 and Alexei Grigorievich Bobrinsky born April 11 1762 (both fathered by Count Grigory Grigoreyevich Orlov). However her heir, the future Emperor Paul I, may also have been illegitimate. The boy, born October 1 1754, was officially fathered by Catherine's husband, Peter III, but she claimed he was actually the son of her lover, Count Serge Saltykov.

—

THE FATE OF 'BASTARD' MOTHERS

When in favour, the women who gave birth to Royal bastards were courted and cosseted, fawned upon and feted. But what happened once they'd been usurped, rejected or their Regal benefactor had expired? While some were well provided for and others married off, an unfortunate number were left to fend for themselves and their semi-regal offspring – with not always happy results. . .

Alice Perrers. Edward III was besotted with his mistress Alice, the mother of his three illegitimate children. She was, however, banished from the Royal household in 1376 for promoting lawsuits in favour of her friends. She returned in 1377, following a dying plea from her lover King but when he died she was banished once more. However Alice was a shrewd business woman and had built up an extensive portfolio of land and manor houses. She died in Essex in 1400.

Katherine Swynford, the mistress of Plantagenent Prince, John of Gaunt, a son of Edward III, was more than well-provided for. She gave birth to four illegitimate children by her Royal lover – John (born 1373), Henry (born 1374), Thomas (born 1377) and Joan (born 1379) – all of whom were given the name Beaufort. Having been widowed twice, John, now Duke of Lancaster, finally married Katherine in 1396 and the four children, now grown up, were legitimized by King Richard II but barred from inheriting the throne. However from eldest child John, descended a granddaughter, Margaret Beaufort, whose son, Henry, would nevertheless successfully claim the throne in 1485 and be crowned Henry VII. As for Katherine? After John of Gaunt's death in 1399, she was known as the Dowager Duchess of Lancaster and died four years later in 1403.

Bessie Blount. The mother of Henry VIII's only acknowledged illegitimate child, Henry Duke of Richmond (born June 15 1519), after which her relationship with the King came to an end. Still a young woman, Bessie was married in 1522 to Gilbert Gilbert Tailboys, 1st Baron Tailboys of Kymeoff, and had three further children. Gilbert left her comfortably off when he died in 1530, and between 1533 and 1535, she married Edward Fiennes, 9th Baron Clinton. They had three daughters. Her Royal bastard, Henry, Duke of Richmond, died of consumption in 1536. For a short while, Bessie was a lady-in-waiting to Henry's fourth wife, Anne of Cleves, but left the Queen's service due to health problems, most likely consumption. She died in 1540.

Lucy Waters. Life was hard for Lucy, the mother of Charles II's beloved son James Monmouth (born April 9 1649), once the King-in-exile severed all contact with her in 1651. She was pensioned-off but Lucy became something of a loose cannon, neglecting the education of James, threatening to expose the fact that she and Charles had, in fact, married (it was never proved), and creating general scandal across Europe. Charles, his mother and sister became alarmed at her neglect of James. Royal advisors kidnapped the boy at least twice and took many of Lucy's papers. After the first time, Lucy got the little boy back, but in December 1657 the boy was taken again and given to the Queen Mother, Henrietta Maria, who became responsible for his upbringing and put him in school at Port-Royal near Paris. Lucy's objections were finally subdued by the Charles threatening to disown the boy if she tried to get him back. Less than a year later, she died in Paris, where she had moved - presumably to be close to her son.

Barbara Palmer, Duchess of Cleveland. At the height of her powers as Charles II's mistress, the fiery-tempered Duchess of Cleveland was referred to as '*the uncrowned Queen.*' But ultimately the King fell out of love with her, even though she'd borne six of his illegitimate children. Charles continued to pay for Barbara and their children on a permanent basis. She took other lovers, including an acrobat and also her second cousin, John Churchill, the future first Duke of Malborough, but she remained on friendly terms with Charles and was seen dining with him a week before his death in February 1685. Barbara continued to attract scandal until her own death in October 1709 – one lover tried to poison her children and she ended up marrying a bigamist who tried to steal her money.

Nell Gwynn. 'Let not poor Nelly starve', was Charles II's death bed plea to his brother, James. To give James II his due, he did just that, paying off most of Nell's debts and bequeathing her a substantial yearly pension. He also paid off the mortgage on Gwyn's Nottinghamshire Lodge in the village of Bestwood, which remained in the Beauclerk family until 1940. Nell herself died in 1687 in the Pall Mall mansion Charles had bought for her.

Clementia Walkinshaw. The mistress of Charles Edward Stuart, aka Bonnie Prince Charlie, and mother of his daughter Charlotte (born October 29 1753), was badly treated by the exiled would-be monarch. Their eight year relationship was extremely volatile with the alcoholic Charles Edward beating and abusing her. Unable to take anymore, Clementina left with her daughter but her former lover refused to make provision for either her or young Charlotte. Clementina pleaded her case to the Prince's father,

James Stuart (the Old Pretender) who settled a yearly allowance upon her but when James died in 1766, Clementia was again left destitute.

Marie Waleska. It is thought Napoleon was already 'going off' his married mistress, Marie Waleska when she became pregnant by him in 1809. By the time the Polish beauty had given birth to his son, Alexandre, on May 4 1810, their relationship was over. The Emperor was, however, extremely generous towards his child's mother. He had her home in Paris redecorated and refurnished, and bought her another house beside the sea in Boulogne. He provided her with free tickets to every museum, gallery and theatre in Paris, as well as a monthly allowance. When Marie, now divorced from her long suffering husband, and Alexandre visited Napoleon in exile on the island of Elba in 1814, he gave her a substantial lump sum as the allowance was no longer valid. In 1816 Marie married again and had another son. She died in 1817 of kidney failure.

Dorothea Jordan. The mother of 10 of William IV's 11 illegitimate children, famous actress Dorothea was, ultimately, very harshly treated by her Royal common law husband. In 1811 he ended their relationship of 21 years as he needed to marry, enter the 'Hymen War

Terrific' and try to begat a legitimate heir. William retained custody of their five sons while giving his ex custody of their five daughters plus a yearly allowance of £4400 (worth almost £250,000 today). In order to retain custody and her money, William stated that she must not return to the stage. However three years later, a son-in-law (the husband of one of Dorothea's daughters from a previous relationship) became heavily in debt and Dorothea returned to the stage to help pay off his creditors. Once the Duke received word of this, he removed their remaining daughters from her care, and stopped her yearly allowance. She fled to France in 1815 and died in poverty a year later.

Did You Know?

It's estimated that half of Britain's aristocracy is descended from illegitimate Royal issue - and you could be, too! 'The Royal Bastards' (www.royalbastard.org) is a society for the descendants of the Illegitimate Sons and Daughters of the Kings of Britain. It is a mathematical certainty that everyone of native English blood is descended from King Edward III (born November 13 1312, died June 21 1377) by at least one bloodline, legitimate and illegitimate. Useful sites for help in ascertaining whether you have blue blood include: www.royal-family-tree.co.uk, www.royalblood.co.uk, and www.burkespeerage.com

BIRTHDAY
CALENDAR

————

Who is your
Royal 'Twin'?

January

1   *Henry, Duke of Cornwall (1511)*, the birth of this son of Henry VIII and Catherine of Aragon, known *'the New Year's Boy'*, was marked with joyous celebrations. But he died before he was seven-weeks-old.

2   *Queen Emma of Hawaii (1836)*, Queen Consort of King Kamehameha IV, from 1856 to his death in 1863.

3   *Emperor Tsuchimikado of Japan (1196)*, the 83rd Emperor of Japan, according to the traditional order of succession.

4   *Malietoa Tanumafili II, King of West Samoa (1913)*, reigned from 1962 until his death in 2007.

5   *Juan Carlos I (1938)*, the current King of Spain.

6   *Richard II of England (1367)*, came to the throne when only 10-years-old and was always in the shadow of his popular father, the Black Prince, who had died the year before. Overthrown by his cousin, the future Henry IV, in 1399.

7   *Princess Charlotte of Wales (1796)*, the *'immense girl'* who somehow came into being despite the fact that her parents, the future George IV and Caroline of Brunswick, hated each other. Great Britain mourned for days after she died in November 1817.

8   *Prince Vincent of Denmark* and *Princess Josephine of Denmark (2011)*, third and fourth children respectively of Crown Prince Frederik of Denmark and his wife, the Australian-born Crown Princess Mary. Prince Vincent was born at 10.30am local time and his twin sister, 26 minutes later.

9   *Kate Middleton, Duchess of Cambridge (1982)*, world's most famous new mum.

10   *Princess Elizabeth of Great Britain (1741)*, a grandchild of George II and sister of George III who died from an inflammation of the bowels when she was 18-years-old.

11   *Prince Carol Ferdinand of Romania (2010)*, born in Bucharest, the baby with the 60-year-old mother and the first royal birth in Eastern Europe in 90 years.

12   *Charles Emmanuel I, Duke of Savoy (1562)* nicknamed *'Head of Fire'* for his rashness and military attitude.

13   *Prince Arthur of Connaught (1883)*, one of Queen Victoria's grandson/ godsons, his parents were Prince Arthur and Princess Louise Margaret of Prussia, Duke and Duchess of Connaught. He was the first Royal Prince to be educated at Eton College.

14   *Mehmed VI (1861)*, 36th and last Sultan of the Ottoman Empire, reigning from 1918 to 1922. On his ninth birthday he was ceremonially circumcised in the special Circumcision Room of the Topkapı Palace in Istanbul.

15   *Princess Michael of Kent (1945)*, Princess *'Pushy'* becomes a granny this year when daughter-in-law, actress Sophie Winkleman, wife of Lord Frederick Windsor, gives birth.

16   *Edmund Crouchback, (1245)* son of Henry III of England and Eleanor of Provence, and named after St Edmund, whose name Eleanor yelled out during labour.

17   *Elizabeth FitzClarence (1801)*, illegitimate daughter of William IV by Dorothea Jordan, and great, great, great, great grandmother of British Prime Minister David Cameron.

18   *Anna Pavlovna of Russia (1795)*, Russian Princess-turned-Queen Consort of the Netherlands who turned down Napoleon Bonaparte's marriage proposal.

19 *Francis II of France (1544)*, born 11 long years after the wedding of his father, the future Henry II of France and Catherine de Medici, his grandfather and namesake Francis I was at the birth – but then he'd been at his parents' wedding night, too.

20 *Sophie, Duchess of Wessex (1965)*, former PR Girl Sophie Rhys Jones who married Prince Edward in 1999, an ectopic pregnancy in 2001 nearly killed her.

21 *Princess Ingrid Alexandra of Norway (2004)*, elder child and only daughter of Crown Prince Haakon of Norway and second in the line of succession to the Norwegian throne.

22 *Prince Christian of Schleswig-Holstein (1831)*, a son-in-law of Queen Victoria, in 1891 he was blinded in one eye after being accidentally shot by Queen Victoria's son, Prince Arthur, while out hunting. His party piece was removing his glass eye at the dinner table.

23 *Princess Caroline of Monaco (1957)*, elder daughter of Princess Grace and Prince Rainier, and conceived on their honeymoon.

24 *Hadrian*, Roman emperor *(76 AD)*, built the famous wall between England and Scotland, and rebuilt the Pantheon in Rome.

25 *Princess Charlene of Monaco (1978)*, South African former Olympic swimmer who married current ruler of the principality, Prince Albert.

26 *Emperor Go-Nara of Japan (1497)*, the 105th Emperor of Japan, according to the traditional order of succession.

27 *Kaiser Wilhelm II (1859)*, eldest of Queen Victoria's 40 grandchildren whose birth was so traumatic, his left arm was deformed.

28 *Henry VII of England (1457)*, first Tudor on the throne, his mother Margaret Beaufort almost died giving birth to him.

29   *George FitzClarence* (*1794*), eldest illegitimate son of William IV by Dorothea Jordan, and his father's favourite.

30   *Adolphus FitzGeorge* (*1846*), second son of Prince George, Duke of Cambridge (Queen Victoria's cousin) and actress Sarah Fairbrother, he became a Rear Admiral in the Royal Navy.

31   *Carole Middleton* (*1955*), mother of Kate and grandmother of baby 'Cambridge'.

February

1   *Princess Stephanie of Monaco* (*1965*), she did not reveal the identity of her third child's father on the birth certificate although he's thought to be former Palace guard, Jean-Raymond Gottlieb.

2   *Nell Gwynn* (*1650*), actress and Orange girl mistress of King Charles II and mother of two of his illegitimate sons

3   *Princess Marie of Saxe-Weimar-Eisenach, Princess of Prussia* (*1808*), loathed her younger sister, Augusta, for being married to the Crown Prince of Prussia while she had to make do with a mere Prince!

4   *Emperor Norton* (*1819*), aka Joshua Abraham Norton, self-proclaimed Emperor of the USA!

5   *Mary, Crown Princess of Denmark* (*1972*), born in Australia and now mother of four.

6   *Queen Anne* (*1665*), 17 pregnancies but not one child survived to adulthood.

7   *Empress Matilda* (*1102*), Princess of England and rightful heir of her father, Henry I; *Puyi. Last Emperor of China* (*1906*), who was breast-fed by wet nurses until he was eight-years-old.

8   *Afonso IV, King of Portugal* (*1291*), the only legitimate heir who was forced to do battle with his father's illegitimate sons.

9   *Princess Raiyah bint Al Hussein of Jordan* (*1986*), works in Japan and regularly features on lists of the world's 'Hot Young Royals'.

10 *Christine Marie of France* (*1606*), elder sister of Charles I's Queen, Henrietta Maria, and jealous of her younger sister's higher status.

11 *Elizabeth of York* (*1465*), daughter of Edward IV, wife of Henry VII and mother of Henry VIII.

12   *Francis II, Holy Roman Emperor* (*1768*), '*spoiled mother's child*' who became the last Holy Roman Emperor, he went on to have four wives and 13 children.

13   *Prince Waldemar of Prussia* (*1868*), favourite son of Vicky, eldest daughter of Victoria and Albert, who died of diphtheria aged 11.

14   *Maria Pia of Savoy* (*1847*), a daughter of Victor Emmanuel II of Italy and Adelaide of Austria, on the day of her baptism, Pope Pius IX, her godfather, gave her a Golden Rose.

15   *Louis XV, King of France* (*1710*), born during the reign of his great-grandfather Louis XIV, he became King in 1715, following the deaths of his great-grandfather, grandfather, father and brother, After his relationship with his favourite mistress Madame de Pompadour became platonic in 1750, he became notoriously promiscuous and a succession of young girls were secretly procured for him.

16   *Grand Duchess Maria Pavlovna of Russia* (*1786*), daughter of Tsar Paul I and grand daughter of Catherine The Great, Maria's face was disfigured as a result of a pioneering application of the Smallpox vaccine and, as a result, her grandmother said it would better if she'd been born a boy.

17   *Princess Helena, Duchess of Albany* (*1861*), married to Victoria's haemophiliac son, Leopold. Gave birth to his son in July 1884, four months after Leopold's death.

18   *Queen Mary I* (*1516*), '*Bloody Mary*' who had two 'phantom' pregnancies.

19   *Prince Andrew, the Duke of York* (*1960*), pee'd on his nanny before his christening.

20   *Louise, Princess Royal, Duchess of Fife* (*1867*), third child and first daughter of the future Edward VII and Queen Alexandra, who had suffered greatly from rheumatic fever while carrying Louise.

21   *Tsar Peter III of Russia* (*1728*), impotent, infantile husband of the future
      Catherine the Great who, having had him assassinated, succeeded him to
      the Russian throne in 1762.

22   *Charles VII, King of France* (*1403*), his legitimacy as French Monarch was
      initially questioned by English Henry VI, as his father Charles VI, known
      as '*The Mad*', disowned him in 1420 and recognized English Henry V and
      his heirs as the legitimate successors.

23   *Arabella Churchill* (*1648*), mistress of James II of England and mother of
      four of his 'natural' children.

24   *Charles V, Holy Roman Empire* (*1500*), eldest son of Philip the Handsome
      and Joanna the Mad.

25   *Princess Alice of Battenburg* (*1885*), mother of the present Duke of
      Edinburgh. Became a nun in her later years.

26   *Prince Ernest August of Hanover* (*1955*), estranged husband of Princess
      Caroline of Monaco.

27   *Constantine I, Roman Emperor* (*272*), the first Christian Emperor of
      Rome.

28   *Margaret of Scotland, Queen of Norway* (*1261*), daughter of Alexander III
      of Scotland, she married Eric II of Norway when she was 20 and he was 13.

29   *James Ogilvy* (*1964*), son of Princess Alexandra, and the first of the four
      Royal babies to be born in 1964,

March

Queen Caroline (*1683*), clever consort of George II who hated her firstborn son, Frederick.

Robert II, King of Scotland (*1316*), born by first known Royal c-section after the death of his mother.

Frederica of Mecklenburg-Strelitz (*1778*), married Earnest Augustus of Hanover, the fifth son of George III, and became Queen of Hanover and Duchess of Cumberland. Earnest's mother, Queen Charlotte, was also Frederica's aunt but she never approved of the marriage as Frederica had been divorced - her ex husband citing her '*loose behaviour*'. Years previously she'd also jilted Earnest's younger brother, Adolphus.

Henry Carey (*1526*), may well have been Henry VIII's illegitimate son by mistress Mary Boleyn. He was said to greatly resemble the KIng.

Henry II of England (*1133*), fiery first Plantagenet King of England who was bow-legged from riding, but handsome with a piercing stare.

John of Gaunt, 1st Duke of Lancaster (*1340*), third surviving son of Edward III and Philippa of Hainault, he was born in Ghent, Belgium, translated into English as 'Gaunt'. He became unpopular in later life and a rumour started that he was actually the son of a Ghent butcher – it made him furious.

Antony Armstrong-Jones, 1st Earl of Snowdon (*1930*), photographer husband of Princess Margaret – the marriage ended in divorce in 1978 with accusations of infidelity on both sides.

Henry FitzClarence (*1797*), one of William IV's illegitimate sons by Dorothea Jordan.

Emperor Go-Nijō (*1285*), the 94th emperor of Japan, according to the traditional order of succession.

10 **Prince Edward** *(1964)*, Earl of Wessex and Elizabeth II's youngest son.

11 **Bodawpaya, Burmese King** *(1745)*, sixth king of the Konbaung Dynasty of Burma, he fathered 62 sons and 58 daughters by approximately 200 consorts.

12 **Anne Hyde** *(1637)*, English wife of James II of England when Duke of York who was subject to bullying by courtiers while in labour with her first child. They didn't believe her child had been fathered by James.

13 **Emperor Joseph II of the Holy Roman Empire** *(1741)*, brother and marriage councilor to Marie Antoinette.

14 **Prince Albert of Monaco** *(1958)*, father of at least two 'natural' children.

15 **Margaret of England, Duchess of Brabant** *(1275)*, 10th child of King Edward I of England and his first wife, Eleanor of Castile. She married John II, Duke of Brabant and moved to Europe when she was 15 but remained her father's favourite. Edward lavished jewellery on her and awarded the messenger who brought him news of her son's arrival with £100.

16 **Napoléon, Prince Imperial of France** *(1856)*, the only child of Emperor Napoleon III of France and his Empress Eugenie. His early death in Africa in 1879 sent shock waves through Europe as he was the last hope for the restoration of the Bonapartes to the throne of France.

17 **James IV of Scotland** *(1473)*, married Margaret Tudor and was a successful King although his reign ended in death at the Battle of Flodden Field in 1513. He was the last monarch from not only Scotland, but also from all of Great Britain, to be killed in battle.

18 **Mary Tudor, Queen of France** *(1496)*, Henry VIII's favourite, younger sister, he named his daughter by Catherine of Aragon after her. She married the ageing King of France who died three months after their

1514 wedding. The beautiful young widow then returned to England and insisted on marrying her true love, Charles Brandon, Duke of Suffolk.

19   **Princess Louisa of Great Britain** (*1749*), delicate younger sister of George III, she died aged 18.

20   **Napoléon II** (*1811*), Napoleon I's only legitimate son by second wife, Marie Louise of Austria whom he proclaimed 'King of Rome'.

21   **Amelia FitzClarence** (*1807*), youngest 'natural' daughter of William IV by Dorothea Jordan.

22   **Hedwig Elisabeth Charlotte of Holstein-Gottorp** (*1759*), Queen Consort of Charles XIII of Sweden, and a famed diarist, memoirist and wit. Also noted for her beauty, at the time of her marriage in 1774 her waist measured just 19 inches.

23   **Princess Eugenie** (*1990*), younger daughter of Prince Andrew and Sarah, Duchess of York.

24   **Ernst, Elector of Saxony** (*1441*), founder of the Ernestine line of Saxon Princes, ancestor of George I of Great Britain, Prince Albert of Saxe-Coburg and Gotha, as well as his wife and cousin Queen Victoria of the United Kingdom, and their cousins Leopold II of Belgium and Empress Charlotte of Mexico.

25   **Blanche of Lancaster** (*1345*), first wife of John of Gaunt and the mother of King Henry IV of England.

26   **Prince George, Duke of Cambridge** (*1819*), legitimate grandson of George III, cousin of Queen Victoria and uncle of Queen Mary, he married actress Sarah Fairbrother in contravention of the Royal Marriages Act when she was pregnant with the third of their three sons. As a result, none of the boys held Royal titles and were ineligible to succeed to the Dukedom of Cambridge - leaving it free for new dad William.

27 **King Louis XVII of France** (*1785*), the younger son of Louis XVI and Marie Antoinette, he died from illness at 10-years-old, his parents having been executed two years earlier. He was never officially crowned King nor did he rule. His title was bestowed by his royalist supporters.

28 **Empress Xiaozhuangwen of the Qing Dynasty** (*1613*), a concubine of the Qing Dynasty ruler Hong Taiji, who was declared his spouse and Empress in 1636.

29 **Isla Phillips** (*2012*), second great grandchild of Elizabeth II, second grandchild of Princess Anne, younger daughter of Peter and Autumn Phillips.

30 *Mehmed II, Ottoman Emperor* (*1482*), known as Sultan Mehmed the Conquerer, he conquered Constantinople and brought an end to the Byzantine Empire, transforming the Ottoman state into an Empire. He is a national hero in Turkey and Istanbul's Fatih Sultan Mehmet Bridge is named after him.

31 **Henri II of France** (*1519*), husband of the potion-making Catherine de Medici who much preferred being the lover of Diane de Poitiers.

A PRIL

1   **Emperor Go-Saga of Japan** (*1220*), 88th ruler of the Japanese Chrysanthemum Dynasty.

2   **Prince George of Denmark** (*1653*), Prince Consort of Queen Anne of England.

3   **King Henry IV of England** (*1367*), his father John of Gaunt married the former governess of his sisters, Katherine Swynford.

4   **Roman Emperor Marcus Aurelius Severus Antoninus Augustus** (*188 AD*), known as '*Caracalla*', referring to the Gallic hood he always wore, he was violent and obsessed with Alexander the Great. Legend has it he was Bassianus, King of the Britons.

5   **Princess Victoria of Hesse** (*1863*), daughter of Princess Alice who was a daughter of Queen Victoria, baby Victoria was born in the same Windsor Castle room as her mother, Alice. Her grandmama witnessed the proceedings. Victoria of Hesse ultimately became the maternal grandmama of Prince Philip, Duke of Edinburgh.

6   **Prince Alexander John** (*1871*), third son of the future Edward VII and Queen Alexandra who lived for just one day.

7   **Prince Leopold, Duke of Albany** (*1853*), Queen Victoria's haemophiliac third son whom she gave birth to under the influence of '*blessed chloroform*', thus sanctioning the use of anesthesia in childbirth.

8   **Christian IX, King of Denmark** (*1818*), unsuccessfully wooed Queen Victoria but later became known as '*the father-in-law of Europe*', as his six children married into other Royal houses. Most current European monarchs are descended from him, including Queen Elizabeth II of the United Kingdom, King Albert II of Belgium, King Harald V of Norway, Queen Margrethe II of Denmark and Grand Duke Henri of Luxembourg.

Consorts Prince Philip, Duke of Edinburgh, and Queen Sofía of Spain are also descendants of Christian IX.

9   **James, Duke of Monmouth** (*1649*), best-loved bastard son of King Charles II by Lucy Waters.

10   **James V of Scotland** (*1512*), father of Mary Queen of Scots who suffered a breakdown and died six days after his daughter's birth in 1542.

11   **Alexei Grog** (*1762*), one of Catherine the Great's illegitimate sons.

12   **Princess Viktoria of Prussia** (*1866*), fifth child of British Princess Victoria, the eldest daughter of Victoria and Albert, and described as '*a kind of wild, Scandinavian woman, with much of her mother's impetuosity*.'

13   **Catherine de' Medici** (*1599*), Italian born Queen consort to Henry II of France, who drilled holes in the floor to spy on her husband with his mistress and also daubed herself with disgusting poultices in the vain hope that she would get pregnant.

14   **Princess 'Baby' Beatrice** (*1857*), ninth and final child of Queen Victoria and Prince Albert.

15   **James Middleton** (*1987*), brother of Kate and uncle to baby Cambridge.

16   **Princess Eléonore of Belgium** (*2008*), the second daughter and fourth child of Prince Philippe of Belgium, Duke of Brabant, the heir apparent to the throne of Belgium, and his wife Princess Mathilde.

17   **Taksin, King of Thailand** (*1734*), son of a Chinese tax collector who was adopted by the Prime Minister and went on to become King of the Thais.

18   **Hayah bint Hamzah, Princess of Jordan** (*2007*), the daughter and only child of Prince Hamzah and Princess Noor bint Asem bin Nayef who divorced in 2009. She is USA-born Queen Noor's second granddaughter.

19   **Ferdinand I of Austria** (*1793*), as a result of his parents' genetic closeness (they were double first cousins), Ferdinand suffered from epilepsy, hydrocephalus, neurological problems, a speech impediment and was incapable of consummating his marriage to his wife, Maria Anna of Sardinia.

20   **Napoleon III** (*1808*), Napoleon Bonaparte's nephew and heir, ruler of the second French Empire and France's last monarch.

21   **Elizabeth II** (*1926*).

22   **Isabella of Castile** (*1451*), mother of Catherine of Aragon and Joanna the Mad, wife of Ferdinand of Aragon and patron of Christopher Columbus.

23   **Malcolm IV of Scotland** (*1141*), nicknamed *'The Maiden'* on the grounds of his chastity - he never married - and his piety, he founded several religious establishments.

24   **Princess Iman bint Al Hussein** (*1983*), half sister of King Abdullah of Jordan and a vet by profession.

25   **Edward II** (*1284*), as a baby he didn't see his parents for two years.

26   **Pedro II of Portugal** (*1648*), locked up his insane brother, then married his sister-in-law.

27   **King Willem Alexander of the Netherlands** (*1967*), his mother, the former Queen Beatrix, abdicated in April 2013 so he could become the ruling Monarch.

28   **Edward IV** (*1442*), the possibly illegitimate King of England.

29   **Alexander II of Russia** (*1818*), freed the serfs when he became Tsar.

30   **Mary II of Great Britain** (*1662*), ruled with husband and first cousin, William III.

M A Y

---

1   **Lady Sarah Chatto** (*1964*), daughter of Princess Margaret and Elizabeth II's niece.

2   **Catherine the Great of Russia** (*1792*), the most renowned and longest-ruling empress of Russia (a reign of 34 years), and famous for her many lovers.

3   **Cecily Neville** (*1417*), mother of Edward IV and Richard III; **Autumn Phillips** (*1978*), Canadian wife of Peter Phillips.

4   **Count Alexandre Joseph Colonna-Waleski** (*1810*), illegitimate son of Napoleon by Marie Waleski and the proof that Napoleon wasn't impotent.

5   **Eugénie de Montijo** (*1826*), wife of Napoleon III and the last Empress of France.

6   **Ferdinand III, Grand Duke of Tuscany** (*1769*), in 1792 during the French Revolution, he became the first monarch to formally recognize the n First Republic, and attempted to work peacefully with it.

7   **Princess Frederica Charlotte of Prussia** (*1767*), the only child of her parents – the Crown Prince and Princess of Prussia - whose union was extremely unhappy due to their mutual infidelities. Her own 1791 marriage to Prince Frederick, Duke of York and Albany, the second son of George III of Great Britain wasn't much happier. The couple soon separated and the Duchess retired to Oatlands Park, Weybridge, where she lived eccentrically with her many dogs. Their relationship after separation appears to have been amicable, but there was never any question of reconciliation. They had no children and Frederica died in 1820.

8   **Charles Beauclerk** (*1670*), illegitimate son of Charles II by Nell Gwynn, the '*little bastard*' who became the first Duke of St Albans.

9   **Maharana Pratap** (*1540*), a Hindu Rajput ruler of Mewar, a region in north-western India in the present day state of Rajasthan.

10   **Claudius II** (*213 AD*), Roman Emperor of barbarian birth who worked his way up the military hierarchy until his troops proclaimed him Emperor in 268 AD.

11   **Anne of Bohemia** (*1366*), much loved Queen of Richard II of England despite the fact that she didn't have children.

12   **Augustus II the Strong of Poland** (*1670*), sired over 300 illegitimate children.

13   **Maria Theresa** (*1717*), Holy Roman Empress, mother of Marie Antoinette and the only female ruler of the Hapsburg dominions.

14   **Margaret of Valois** (*1553*), the only one of Catherine de Medici and Henry II's 10 children who enjoyed good health.

15   **Zara Phillips Tindall** (*1981*), show jumping daughter of Princess Anne.

16   **Sorry - you don't have a Royal twin!**

17   **Caroline of Brunswick** (*1768*), consort of George IV who loathed her and her '*soiled hind quarters*.'

18   **Nicholas II of Russia** (*1868*), the last Tsar of Russia, murdered by the Bolsheviks in 1917.

19   **Queen Charlotte** (*1744*), consort of George III of England, mother of 15 children and almost continuously pregnant from 1761 to 1783.

20   **Prince Albert Kamehameha of Hawaii** (*1858*), named Albert Edward in honour of Albert Edward, Prince of Wales, the future King Edward VII, Queen Victoria agreed to become his godmother by proxy and sent an

elaborate silver christening cup but tragically four-year-old Albert died four days after the baptism.

21 **Philip II of Spain** (*1527*), during his four year marriage to Queen Mary I of England, he was King of England and Ireland and pretender to the Kingdom of France.

22 **Princess Elizabeth of Great Britain** (*1770*), the seventh child and third daughter of King George III and Queen Charlotte, who is said to have borne an illegitimate daughter, Eliza, in 1788.

23 **Philip I of France** (*1052*), known as 'Philip the Amorous', he divorced his first wife Bertha on the grounds that she was too fat - he was excommunicated as a result.

24 **Queen Victoria** (*1819*), described by her father, the Duke of Kent, as a *pocket Hercules'* when first born.

25 **Princess Helena of the United Kingdom** (*1846*), the third daughter and fifth child of the reigning British monarch, Queen Victoria, and her husband Prince Albert, and born the day after her mother's 27th birthday. Albert reported to his brother, Ernest II, the Duke of Saxe-Coburg and Gotha, that Helena *'came into this world quite blue, but she is quite well now.'*

26 **Queen Mary** (*1867*), consort of George V who found it hard to show her six children affection.

27 **William II, Prince of Orange** (*1626*), who married Mary Henrietta, Princess Royal, the eldest daughter of King Charles I of England and Henrietta Maria of France. Their son became William III of England.

28 **George I** (*1660*), the *'Pig-Snout'* first Hanoverian King who had his wife placed under house arrest when he discovered she'd had an affair.

29 **Charles II** (*1630*), the womanising King who lost his virginity to his wet-nurse!

30   **Princess Caroline of Great Britain** (*1713*). the fourth child and third daughter of George II and Queen Caroline, who never married. According to popular opinion, she was lovesick for married-but-bisexual courtier, Lord Hervey, who may have had an affair with Caroline's elder brother, Prince Frederick!

31   **Margaret Beaufort** (*1443*), Tudor matriarch and mother of Henry VII who gave birth to him aged 13.

JUNE

1   **Thomas Brotherton** (*1300*), son of King Edward I of England and his second wife Margaret of France, and named after St Thomas Beckett whose name the Queen had cried out during labour.

2   **Constantine II of Greece** (*1940*), King of Greece from 1964 until the abolition of the monarchy in 1973. Godfather to Prince William, Duke of Cambridge.

3   **King George V** (*1865*), shocked his grandmother Queen Victoria by taking all his clothes off when she ordered him to sit under the tea table for being naughty. He was only three at the time.

4   **George III of Great Britain** (*1738*), born two months premature and christened the day of his birth as he was not expected to survive. He lived for another 81 years.

5   **Edmund of Langley, 1st Duke of York, 1st Earl of Cambridge** (*1341*), was a younger son of King Edward III of England and Philippa of Hainault, the fourth of their five sons who lived to adulthood. Like so many medieval Princes, Edmund gained his identifying nickname from his birthplace of Langley, now Kings Langley, in Hertfordshire.

6   **Alexandra, last Tsarina of Russia** (*1872*), the not-so-Sunny grand daughter of Queen Victoria – her mother was Princess Alice, the Queen's second daughter – who tragically inherited the haemophiliac carrying gene from her mother.

7   **Carlota of Mexico** (*1840*), born Charlotte of Belgium, daughter of Louise Marie of Orleans and King Leopold of Belgium (Queen Victoria's uncle), the baby girl was named after her father's first wife, Princess Charlotte of Wales, who had died in childbirth in 1817. She married Maximilian of Austria, later Emperor of Mexico.

8   **Andrea Casiraghi** (*1984*), eldest son of Caroline, Princess of Monaco and Hanover, second in line to the Monegasque crown and likely to succeed to the throne if his uncle, Prince Albert, dies without legal issue. He and his girlfriend welcomed their first child into the world on March 21 2013.

9   **Peter the Great** (*1726*), abnormally tall Russian emperor – 6 ' 8" – who modernized his country into a major European power.

10   **Prince Philip, Duke of Edinburgh** (*1921*), the baby born on a Corfu kitchen table.

11   **Anne Neville** (*1456*), an English noblewoman, the daughter of Richard Neville, 16th Earl of Warwick '*The Kingmaker*', who became Princess of Wales as the wife of Edward of Westminster, and then Queen of England as the consort of King Richard III.

12   **Emperor Gaozong** (*1107*), born Zhao Gou, Gaozong was the 9th son of Emperor Huizong and the younger half-brother of Emperor Qinzong. His mother was a concubine who later became Empress Dowager.

13   **Charles the Bald** (*839*), Holy Roman Emperor and King of West Francia, it's likely that Charles' nickname was ironic – he was not bald but extremely hairy.

14   **Sophia Dorothea Ulrica Alice of Prussia** (*1870*), grand daughter of Queen Victoria but named after her German family rather than her British one.

15   **Edward, the Black Prince** (*1330*), eldest son and heir of Edward III and known as the '*Black Prince*' because he wore black armour, he became the most feared military commander in Europe but predeceased his father by a year in 1396.

16   **Princess Henrietta Anne** (*1644*), the ninth and youngest child of Charles I and Henrietta Maria who was born in the middle of the English Civil

War. Her father saw her just once before he was executed in 1649 while her mother fled to France alone, not believing the sickly infant would survive the journey. Against the odds she did, and Henrietta Anne, known as Minette, joined her mother there two years later.

17 **Edward I** (*1239*), on the night of his birth, the citizens of London took to the streets and celebrated by torchlight.

18 **Charles Fitzroy, 2nd Duke of Cleveland** (*1662*), eldest of Charles II's illegitimate sons by mistress Barbara Villiers.

19 **James I of England and VI of Scotland** (*1566*), only son of Mary Queen of Scots who inherited the English throne in 1603; **Wallis Simpson, Duchess of Windsor** (*1896*), Edward VIII relinquished the throne for her.

20 **Birgitte, Duchess of Gloucester** (*1946*), Danish-born secretary who married Prince Richard of Gloucester (now the Duke) in 1972.

21 **Prince William, Duke of Cambridge** (*1982*), the world's most famous new daddy.

22 **Princess Soraya of Iran** (*1932*), divorced by the Shah because she couldn't have children, died in 2001.

23 **Michael Middleton** (*1949*), father of Kate and baby Cambridge's grandfather; **Edward VIII Duke of Windsor** (*1894*), not '*heir-conditioned*' according to his wife; **The Empress Josephine** (*1763*), divorced because she couldn't give Napoleon children.

24 **Philippa of Hainault** (*1314*), Queen of Edward III of England, gave birth to 13 children and was '*a very good and charming person who exceeded most ladies for sweetness of nature and virtuous disposition.*'

25 **Lord Louis Mountbatten** (*1900*), '*Dickie*', Prince of Battenburg and uncle of the Duke of Edinburgh, he was a great grandson of Queen Victoria, who was also his godmother, and he accidentally knocked off her spectacles before his christening.

26   **Earl of St Andrews** (*1962*), elder son of the current Duke of Kent; **Dorothy Goldsmith** (*1930*), Kate's maternal granny who died in 2006.

27   **Charles IX of France** (*1550*), third son of Henry II of France and Catherine de' Medici, who became King at just 10-years-old when his older brother, Francis II – the young husband of Mary Queen of Scots - died of an ear infection.

28   **Henry VIII** (*1491*).

29   **Maria of Aragon** (*1482*), Queen of Portugal, one sister was Catherine of Aragon, another was Joanna '*The Mad*'. Also had a twin sister who was stillborn.

30   **Charles VIII of France** (*1470*), his godfather was Edward of Westminster, the son of King Henry VI of England who lived in France following the deposition of his father by King Edward IV.

July

1   **Diana, Princess of Wales** (*1961*).

2   **Elizabeth Tudor** (*1492*), baby sister of Henry VIII who died when she was three-years-old and is buried in Westminster Abbey.

3   **Louis XI of France** (*1423*), hated the English but interested in science - he once pardoned a man sentenced to death on condition that he act as a guinea pig for a gallstone operation.

4   **Prince Michael of Kent** (*1942*), born on American Independence Day and has the middle name of Theodore in honour of President Roosevelt, one of his godfathers.

5   **Princess Joan, daughter of Edward II** (*1321*), the baby 'rained on' when she was born in the Tower of London.

6   **Maximilian I of Mexico** (*1832*), born in Vienna, he became the Emperor of Mexico in 1864, but within three years was deposed and executed.

7   **Princess Purnika of Nepal** (*2000*), the eldest daughter of Paras, former Crown Prince of Nepal, third in line to the defunct Nepalese Throne, now lives with her family in Singapore.

8   **Carlos, Prince of Asturias** (*1545*), mentally unstable, physically deformed eldest son of Philip II of Spain. As Carlos's conditioned worsened and he threatened to kill his father, Philip imprisoned him in 1568 and he died in solitary confinement later that year.

9   **Princess Sophie Hélène Béatrice of France** (*1786*), youngest of the four children of Marie Antoinette and Louis XVI, she died at just 11-months-old after suffering convulsions caused by the cutting of new teeth.

10   **Maria Walpole** (*1736*), the 'commoner' wife of Prince William Henry, Duke of Gloucester and Edinburgh, brother of King George III. The

marriage occurred without the knowledge of King George III and led to the passing of the Royal Marriages Act in 1772.

11   **Robert the Bruce** (*1274*), one of Scotland's greatest Kings.

12   **Prince John, fifth son of George V** (*1905*), '*the lost prince*', hidden away due to his epilepsy. He died when he was 13.

13   **Julius Caesar** (*100 BC*).

14   **Abbas II of Egypt** (*1874*), the last Khedive of Egypt and Sudan who, as a child, had a British governess.

15   **Princess Louise Marie of France** (*1737*), youngest of Louis XV's 10 children, she was deeply religious and became a Carmelite nun, believing it would compensate for her father's lax morals.

16   **Cecilia Renata of Austria** (*1611*), she married Władysław IV of Poland and was known for being polite - so polite that when she could not remove her husband's mistress from court, she had the mistress married to a courtier.

17   **Lady Janet Fleming, nee Stewart** (*1502*), an illegitimate daughter of King James IV of Scotland, nanny to Mary Queen of Scots, mistress of King Henry II of France, by whom she had a legitimised son, Henri d'Angoulême; **Camilla, Duchess of Cornwall** (1947).

18   **Isabella of Austria** (*1501*), daughter of Joanna the Mad and Philip the Handsome.

19   **Princess Augusta of Cambridge** (*1822*), her father was Prince Adolphus, Duke of Cambridge, the seventh son of George III, making her a first cousin of Queen Victoria.

20   **Alexander the Great** (*356 BC*), by the age of 30, he had created one of the largest empires of the Ancient world.

21   **Maria Christina of Austria** (*1858*), known to her family as Christa, she was described as '*tall, fair, sensible, and well educated*' and became Queen Consort of Spain.

22   **Joanna/Joan of England, Queen of Scotland** (*1210*), the eldest daughter of King John and Countess Isabella of Angoulême, her widowed mother stole the French Prince she had been betrothed to and she ended up with Alexander II of Scotland.

23   **Haile Selassie I** (*1892*), Emperor of Ethiopia from 1930 to 1974 and heir to a dynasty that traced its origins by tradition from King Solomon and Queen of Sheba.

24   **Princess Charlotte of Prussia** (*1860*), a grand daughter of Queen Victoria, at an early age Charlotte displayed a nervous and agitated personality, frequently biting her nails and tearing at her clothes. In a letter to her daughter Vicky, Charlotte's mother, Queen Victoria wrote, '*tell Charlotte I was appalled to hear of her biting her things. Grandmama does not like naughty girls*'. Charlotte was still being naughty when she grew up. In 2010, a German magazine published new research suggesting that, in 1891, Charlotte hosted orgies in a hunting lodge near Berlin in order to entrap aristocratic rivals.

25   **Princess Louise Margaret of Prussia** (*1860*), her father, Prince Frederick Charles of Prussia, was a double cousin of Princess Charlotte's father, the future German Emperor Friedrich III, whose wife, Vicky (Queen Victoria's eldest), was the sister of Prince Arthur, the man Louise Margaret married in March 1879 at St George's Chapel Windsor!

26   **Joseph I, Holy Roman Emperor** (*1678*), crowned King of Hungary at the age of nine, and King of the Romans aged 11. Died in 1711 aged 43, from smallpox, having previously promised his long-suffering wife he would stop having affairs if he survived.

27   **Ludovico Sforza, Duke of Milan** (*1452*), best known as the man who commissioned Da Vinci's 'The Last Supper'.

28   **Prince Maha Vajiralongkorn** (*1952*), Crown Prince of Thailand and heir apparent to the throne, he has been married three times and has seven children.

29   **Isabel, Princess Imperial of Brazil Dona** (*1846*), born in Rio de Janeiro, the eldest daughter and heiress presumptive of Emperor Dom Pedro II, she married a French Prince and they had three sons. She acted as her father's Regent on occasions but in 1889, her family was deposed in a military coup, and she spent the last 30 years of her life in exile in France.

30   **Prince Hridayendra of Nepal** (*2002*), was the second in line to the Nepal's royal throne until the monarchy was officially abolished on 28 May 2008. He now lives with his family in Singapore.

31   **Phillip III, Duke of Burgundy** (*1396*), known *'Phillip the Good'* as his court flourished during his reign but he also had at least eighteen illegitimate children by various of his 24 documented mistresses.

A UGUST

---

1   **Edmund of Woodstock** (*1301*), the son of Edward I and Margaret of France who, as a little boy, broke his own toy drum.

2   **Philip II, Duke of Orléans** (*1674*), his father was openly gay and is rumoured to have murdered Philip's mother, English Princess Henrietta, who was also a first cousin, when Philip was just six-years-old

3   **Charlotte Casiraghi** (*1986*), the model daughter of Princess Caroline of Monaco and fourth in line to the Grimaldi throne.

4   **Queen Elizabeth, The Queen Mother** (*1900*).

5   **Lady Sophie Windsor (nee Sophie Winkleman)** (*1980*), actress wife of Lord Frederick Windsor. Expecting her first baby in August 2013.

6   **Louise de La Vallière** (*1644*), a mistress of French King Louis XIV who gave birth to four of his illegitimate children.

7   **Princess Amelia** (*1783*), George III's youngest and favourite daughter.

8   **Princess Beatrice of York** (*1988*), born 8/8/88 and almost a caesarean birth.

9   **Eudoxia Lopukhina** (*1669*), first wife of Russia's Peter the Great who banished her to a monastery when he became bored of her.

10   **Madeleine de Valois** (*1520*), daughter of King Francis I of France and the fragile first wife of James V of Scotland.

11   **Anna Maria Luisa de' Medici** (*1667*), her mother, Marguérite Louise d'Orleans, Grand Duchess of Tuscany, deliberately tried to miscarry her.

12   **Tsaretvich Alexei of Russia** (*1904*), the longed-for heir to the Russian throne who tragically suffered from haemophilia.

13   **Alfonso XI of Castile** (*1311*), became King when he was just one-year-old.

14   **Princess Catherine of York** (*1479*), sixth daughter of Edward IV and also sister of Edward V, niece of Richard III, sister-in-law of Henry VII and aunt of Henry VIII.

15   **Napoleon Bonaparte** (*1769*), **Princess Anne, The Princess Royal** (*1950*).

16   **Philippa Plantagenet** (*1355*), grand daughter of Edward III, from whom the House of York was descended.

17   **Prince Richard, 1st Duke of York** (*1473*), the younger 'little Prince' in the Tower.

18   **Ludwika Maria Gonzaga** (*1611*), French Princess and Queen Consort to two Polish Kings.

19   **Elizabeth Stuart, Queen of Bohemia** (*1596*), the eldest daughter of King James I of England, she is the 16 x great grandmother of Elizabeth II.

20   **Prince Gabriel of Belgium** (*2003*), the second child and eldest son of Prince Philippe, Duke of Brabant, the heir apparent to the throne of Belgium, and his wife Princess Mathilde.

21   **Princess Margaret Rose** (*1930*), late sister of Elizabeth II who died in 2002.

22   **Milan I of Serbia** (*1854*), his parents divorced when he was a baby and his own marriage broke up due to his infidelity – he had an affair with Winston Churchill's mother, Jennie Jerome.

23   **Louis XVI** (*1754*), husband of Marie Antoinette who couldn't get it '*up*' or '*in*' for the first seven years of their marriage; **George Seymour Crole** (*1799*), the only illegitimate child recognised by George IV.

24 **Geoffrey Plantagenet** (*1113*), Duke of Anjou and founder of the Plantagenet dynasty; **Alexandre Coste** (*2003*), illegitimate son of Prince Albert of Monaco.

25 **Ivan The Terrible of Russia** (*1530*), Tsar, rapist and mass murderer.

26 **Prince Albert** (*1819*), dearly beloved Consort of Queen Victoria.

27 **Anne Marie of Orléans** (*1669*), Queen of Italy, who from 1714 to 1720, was the heiress presumptive to the Jacobite claim to the thrones of England, Scotland, and Ireland.

28 **George Duke of Buckingham** (*1592*), his closeness to Charles I prevented Royal Wife Henrietta Maria conceiving until his death in 1628.

29 **Maria Anna Sophia of Saxony** (*1728*), one of 15 children yet she had none of her own.

30 **Stuart Arthur Forster** (*1899*), rumoured to be an illegitimate son of Edward VII by an Irish lady, Grace Forster.

31 **Princess Augusta** (*1737*), the '*she-mouse*' baby born on the run.

SEPTEMBER

1   **Elisabeth Richeza of Poland, Queen of Poland** (*1286*), outlived her two Royal Bohemian husbands and finally lived with a lover.

2   **Louis Bonaparte, King of Holland** (*1778*), brother of Napoleon I, father of Napoleon III - keeping his bisexuality secret caused periods of depression and mental illness.

3   **Diane de Poitiers** (*1499*), beloved mistress of Henry II of France, after an evening together she would send him off to do his reluctant conjugal duties with wife, Catherine de Medici.

4   **Alexander III of Scotland** (*1241*), became Scottish monarch at just seven-years-old.

5   **Louis XIV, King of France** (*1638*), '*the unexpected gift of God*' born when his parents had been married 22 years, lothario Louis became known as 'The Sun King' and reigned for 72 years!

6   **Pippa Middleton** (*1983*), aka '*Her Royal Hotness*', younger sister of the Duchess of Cambridge.

7   **Elizabeth I** (*1533*), the Virgin Queen - or was she?

8   **Richard I, The Lionheart** (*1157*), the crusade-loving King.

9   **Victoria Federica de Marichalar y de Borbón** (*2000*), granddaughter of King Juan Carlos I of Spain and named after her great, great grandmother, Victoria Eugenie of Spain who was a grand daughter of Britain's Queen Victoria.

10   **Maria Theresa of Spain** (*1638*), first wife of Louis XIV of France who had no choice but to put up with her husband's many infidelities.

11 **John George of Brandenburg** (*1525*), Prussian Royal Duke who married three times and had 22 legitimate children.

12 **King Francis I of France** (*1494*), voyeuristic pervert who watched his son and daughter-in-law consummate their marriage.

13 **John II Komnenos, Byzantine Emperor** (*1087*), described by contemporaries as *'short and unusually ugly'* but he was pious and dedicated.

14 **Sir Angus Ogilvy** (*1936*), the late husband of Princess Alexandra.

15 **Prince Harry** (*1984*), the world's most eligible bachelor.

16 **Henry V** (*1387*), *'Cry God for Harry, England and St George!'*

17 **Crown Princess Pavlos Marie Chantal of Greece and Denmark** (*1968*), US socialite-turned-Crown Princess, albeit in exile, and mother of five.

18 **Eleanor of Portugal, Holy Roman Empress** (*1434*), chose to marry Holy Roman Emperor Frederick III rather than the French King because she wanted to an Empress rather than a mere Queen.

19 **Henri III of France** (*1551*), Catherine de Medici's fourth and favourite son whom she called *'Chers Jeux'- Precious Eyes.* Thought to be homosexual, he unsuccessfully courted Elizabeth I of England whom he unflatteringly called *'an old creature with a sore leg'*.

20 **Arthur Tudor** (*1486*), eldest son of Henry VII, and Catherine of Aragon's first husband who died in 1502. Arthur's younger brother, the future Henry VIII, was not created Prince of Wales until it was ascertained that Catherine was not pregnant with Arthur's child.

21 **Bertha of Savoy, German Queen and Holy Roman Empire Empress** (*1051*), her womanising husband Henry IV tried to divorce her soon after

their marriage but the Pope would not allow it. They went on to have five children.

22   **Anne of Cleves** (*1515*), Henry VIII's fourth wife whom '*he liketh not*' and subsequently divorced.

23   **Augustus Caesar, Roman Emperor** (*63 BC*), raised by his grandmother Julia who was the sister of Julius Caesar. When Julius Caesar died in 44BC, Augustus learned that he was to be the former Emperor's heir.

24   **Catherine of Saxe-Lauenburg, Queen of Sweden** (*1513*), German born Princess who was unpopular in her adopted country as she refused to learn the language and was also said to be melancholy.

25   **Qianlong, Emperor of China** (*1711*), adored both by his grandfather, the Kangxi Emperor and his father, the Yongzheng Emperor. Some historians argue that the main reason why Kangxi Emperor appointed Yongzheng as his successor was because Qianlong was his favourite grandson.

26   **Anna of Bavaria, Queen of the Romans** (*1329*), Queen consort of Germany, Bohemia and the Romans who died when she was 23.

27   **Louis XIII of France** (*1601*), born with an extreme congenital speech impediment and a double row of teeth, there were rumours he was homosexual although he did manage to become the father of '*the unexpected gift of God*' (see September 5 entry).

28   **Amelie of Orleans** (*1861*), French Princess and last Queen Consort of Portugal who survived the assignation attempt on the Portuguese Royal Family which killed her husband King Carlos I and their eldest son.

29   **Princess Thyra** (*1853*), daughter of Christian IX of Denmark, who secretly gave birth to an illegitimate child.

30   **Princess Maria-Esmeralda of Belgium** (*1956*), half-sister of the current monarch King Albert II, she works as a journalist, writing under the name 'Esméralda de Réthy'.

October

King Henry III (*1207*), crowned at just nine-years-old.

King Richard III (*1452*), much maligned Monarch whose remains were found in a Leicester car park.

Leopold II, Grand Duke of Tuscany (*1797*), the son of double first cousins, Ferdinand III, Grand Duke of Tuscany and Princess Luisa Maria Amelia Teresa of the Two Sicilies.

Prince Emmanuel of Belgium (*2005*), grandson of Albert II and fourth in line to the throne of Belgium after his father and his older sister Elisabeth and brother Gabriel.

Mary Beatrice of Modena (*1658*), second wife of James II who was forced to suffer the indignity of giving birth to her only surviving son, James Francis Edward, in front of a packed birthing chamber, and then had to live with rumour that a changeling child had been smuggled into the room in a warming pan.

Louis Philippe I (*1773*), forced to abdicate in 1848 and lived out his life in exile in England, the last King to rule France, although Emperor Napoleon III was the last monarch.

Princess Senate Seeiso of Lesotho (*2001*), is the eldest child of King Letsie III of Lesotho and his wife Queen Masenate Mohato Seeiso.

Lady Margaret Douglas (*1515*), daughter of Margaret Tudor, dowager Queen of Scotland, and Archibald Douglas, 6th Earl of Angus; mother of Henry, Lord Darnley who married Mary Queen of Scots and therefore the grandmother of James I of England and VI of Scotland.

Prince Edward, Duke of Kent (*1935*), current Duke and Elizabeth II's first cousin.

10   **Mary Plantagenet** (*1344*), daughter of Edward III and Philippa of Hainault, married John of Brittany but never visited there as she died of lethargy some 30 weeks after the 1361 wedding.

11   **Prince Constantijn of the Netherlands** (*1969*), younger son of recently abdicated Queen Beatrix, and a Brussels-based Lawyer.

12   **King Edward VI** (*1537*), the most longed-for heir in Royal history, his mother Jane Seymour was in labour for three days and then died of puerperal or childbirth fever 12 days after his birth.

13   **Edward of Westminster, Prince of Wales** (*1453*), known as the '*child of sorrow and infidelity*' as his father Henry VI suffered from mental illness and there were rumours his mother Margaret of Anjou had been unfaithful in order to get pregnant. He died at the Battle of Tewkesbury in 1471.

14   **James II** (*1633*), handsome but dull, this last British Roman Catholic monarch who lost his throne was known as '*Dismal Jimmy*'.

15   **Sarah Ferguson, Duchess of York** (*1959*), divorced from the Duke but still retains her title.

16   **James II of Scotland** (*1430*), born a twin but by but by his first birthday, his brother had died, making James the heir.

17   **Grand Duchess Maria Alexandrovna of Russia** (*1853*), married Prince Alfred, Victoria's second son, but insisted on keeping her '*Grand Duchess*' status.

18   **Frederick III, German Emperor** (*1831*), had a miserable childhood due to his parents' unhappy marriage but everything changed when he fell in love with – and later married - Princess Victoria, the eldest child of Victoria and Albert.

19   **Empress Myeongseong of Korea** (*1851*), aristocratic orphan who became an Empress.

20   **Pauline Bonaparte** (*1780*), sister of Napoleon I, washer woman-turned-Princess.

21   **George Plantagenet, 1st Duke of Clarence** (*1449*), brother of Kings Edward IV and Richard III, the character in Shakespeare's *Richard III* who drowned in a butt of Malmsey wine.

22   **Dauphin Louis Joseph** (*1781*), son of Marie Antoinette who, she announced shortly after his birth, belonged to France rather than to her.

23   **Peter II of Russia** (*1715*), orphaned grandson of Peter the Great who as a child was kept in the strictest seclusion.

24   **Victoria Eugenie of Battenberg** (*1887*), grand daughter of Queen Victoria and made godmother to her own grandson, Crown Prince Felipe of Spain, shortly before her death in 1969.

25   **Princess Elisabeth of Belgium** (*2001*), second in line to the throne, delivered by caesarian section, weighing six-and-a-half pounds.

26   **Miguel I of Portugal** (*1802*), may have been the result of one of his Spanish mother's adulterous affairs.

27   **Catherine of Valois** (*1401*), wife of Henry V of England and mother of Henry VI, after Henry V's death in 1422, she became the secret wife of Owen Tudor, the mother of Edmund Tudor and therefore the grandmother of the future Henry VII.

28   **Henry III, Holy Roman Emperor** (*1017*), his father-in-law was Canute the Great, King of Denmark, England, and Norway.

29   **Marie of Romania** (*1875*), grand daughter of Queen Victoria who thought she was dying when first pregnant because no one had told her about morning sickness – or how to get pregnant.

30   **Julia the Elder** (*39 BC*), daughter of the Emperor Augustus, stepsister and second wife of the Emperor Tiberius, maternal grandmother of the Emperor Caligula and the Empress Agrippina the Younger, grandmother-in-law of the Emperor Claudius, and maternal great-grandmother of the Emperor Nero.

31   **Sarah Fairbrother** (*1817*), '*Mrs FitzGeorge*', the actress who married Prince George, Duke of Cambridge, contravene to the Royal Marriage Act of 1772, and the mother of his three sons - George, Adolphus and Augustus. She also had an illegitimate son and daughter by previous relationships.

November

1   **Duke Leopold III of Austria** (*1351*), born when his mother was 51.

2   **King Edward V** (*1470*), one of the little Princes thought to have been killed in the Tower of London in 1483; **Marie Antoinette** (*1755*).

3   **David, Viscount Linley** (*1961*), son of Princess Margaret.

4   **King William III, William of Orange** (*1650*), joint ruler of the British throne with his first cousin and wife, Queen Mary II.

5   **Princess Fawzia Fuad of Egypt and Iran** (*1921*), glamorous first wife of the Shah of Persia who, in 1945, obtained an Egyptian divorce as the six year marriage was not a success.

6   **Joanna of Castile** (*1479*), nicknamed 'the Mad', her husband made her pay for the upkeep of their first child because she was a girl.

7   **Constans II, Byzantine Emperor** (*630*), assassinated in his bath aged 37.

8   **Princess Augusta Sophia** (*1768*), the seventh child of George III and Queen Charlotte who was delivered in just 90 minutes; **Kate Jorgenson** (*1871*), the secret child borne to Danish Princess Thyra and immediately adopted.

9   **King George II** (*1683*), he spoke only French until he was four; **King Edward VII** (*1841*), a lack of love in his childhood may explain why he never stopped pursuing the ladies.

10   **Bridget of York** (*1480*), the English Princess-turned-nun.

11   **Gisela of Swabia, German Empress** (*989*), thrice married Gisela stood 5'8" and had long, blonde hair.

12 **Princess Grace of Monaco** (*1929*), former American movie star Grace Kelly.

13 **Edward III** (*1312*), every person of native English blood is descended from this King.

14 **Prince Charles, Prince of Wales** (*1948*).

15 **Peter Phillips** (*1977*), son of Princess Anne and first grandson of Elizabeth II.

16 **Henrietta Maria** (*1609*), wife and Queen consort of Charles I.

17 **Princess Astrid of Sweden, Queen of the Belgians** (*1905*), mother of current King Albert, beautiful Astrid was tragically killed in a car crash when she was just 29, and Albert only 12-months-old.

18 **Wilhelmine of Prussia, Queen of the Netherlands** (*1774*), and great, great, great grandmother of recently abdicated Dutch Queen, Beatrix.

19 **King Charles I** (*1600*), English King who literally lost his head.

20 **Emperor Maximinus of Rome** (*270 AD*), a committed pagan, he engaged in one of the last persecutions of Christians.

21 **Princess Victoria, Empress of Germany** (*1840*), honeymoon baby *'Pussy'* and eldest child of Victoria and Albert.

22 **Marie of Guise** (*1515*), mother of Mary Queen of Scots.

23 **Alphonso X** (*1221*), King of Castile, big brother of English Queen, Eleanor of Castile.

24 **Prince Alphonso** (*1273*), named for his uncle by his mother and father, Queen Eleanor and King Edward I; **the secret illegitimate daughter** of Marie Sophia, Queen of Naples, who was whisked away immediately after birth (*1862*).

25   **Catherine of Braganza** (*1638*), long suffering wife of philandering Charles II.

26   **Princess Maud of Wales** (*1869*), third daughter of Edward VII and first Queen of Norway.

27   **Barbara Palmer** (*1640*), mistress of Charles II and mother of five of his illegitimate children.

28   **Margaret Tudor** (*1479*), elder sister of Henry VIII and wife of James IV of Scotland.

29   **Prince Lionel** (*1338*), first Duke of Clarence and third son of Edward III.

30   **Augusta, Princess of Wales** (*1722*), who was forced to give birth to first child '*The She-Mouse*' on the run.

December

1   **Queen Alexandra** (*1844*), long-suffering wife of Edward VII.

2   **Pedro II of Brazil** (*1825*), became Emperor at just five-years-old and reigned for 58 years.

3   **King Charles VI of France** (*1368*), had bouts of insanity when he believed he was made of glass and also denied he had a wife and children. His eldest daughter Isabella married widower Richard II of England when she was just six-years-old and became his Queen. She refused to marry the future Henry V when Richard died.

4   **Barbara of Portugal** (*1711*), well-educated but plain Portuguese Princess who became a Queen Consort of Spain.

5   **Emperor Jianwen of China** (*1377*), second Emperor of the Ming Dynasty.

6   **King Henry VI** (*1421*), the Lancastrian King with mental health issues.

7   **Lord Darnley** (*1546*), 2nd husband of Mary Queen of Scots and father of James I of Great Britain; **Marie Waleska** (*1786*), mistress of Napoleon and mother of the illegitimate son who proved the Emperor's ability to father a child.

8   **Mary Queen of Scots** (*1542*).

9   **Frederick FitzClarence** (1799), illegitimate son of William IV by Dorothea Jordan.

10   **Daisy Greville,** Countess of Warwick (*1861*), mistress of Edward VII when Prince of Wales whose youngest son, Maynard, born in 1898, was possibly fathered by the Prince.

11   **Kamehameha V of Hawaii** (*1830*), common born and adopted into the Hawaiian Royal family via the ancient tradition of 'hanai'.

12   **Anne of Denmark** (*1574*), wife of James I of Great Britain and mother of Charles I; **Marie Louise of Austria** (*1791*), Napoleon's second wife.

13   **Princes Nicolas and Aymeric** (2005), twin grandsons of Albert II of Belgium - Nicolas is the elder twin

14   **King George VI of Great Britain** (*1895*), as a child his birthday was never properly celebrated because it fell on the day of Prince Albert's death.

15   **Emperor Nero** (*AD 37*), falsely rumoured to have set fire to Rome.

16   **Katherine of Aragon** (*1485*), first wife of Henry VIII.

17   **James Mountbatten Windsor, Viscount Severn,** (*2007*), son of Edward and Sophie, Earl and Countess of Wessex.

18   **Elizabeth, Empress of Russia** (*1709*), encouraged the future Catherine the Great to be unfaithful to her husband, Elizabeth's impotent nephew, in order to get pregnant, and took the baby, Prince Paul, away from Catherine as soon as he was born.

19   **Marie Therese of France** (*1778*), the eldest daughter of Marie Antoinette and Louis XVI of France, her birth date was one of the most eagerly anticipated events in French history as her parents were married for seven years before they conceived her. The birth was witnessed by a crowd who had forced their way into the delivery room, including two chimney sweeps who balanced on top of a cupboard!

20   **Prince George, Duke of Kent** (*1902*), father of the present Duke and uncle of Elizabeth II. Bisexual, drug addiction problems, said to have fathered an illegitimate son, died in an air crash in 1942.

21   **Amalia of Oldenburg** (*1818*), a German princess who became a Greek Queen but couldn't give her husband an heir. A post-mortem carried out after in death in 1875, revealed she had neither uterus nor fallopian tubes.

2 2   **Roger of Sicily** (*1095*), united all the Norman conquests in Italy into one Kingdom and became one of the greatest 12th Century Kings in Europe.

2 3   **Maximillian of Brunswick-Luneberg** (*1666*), younger brother of King George I, whose twin was still-born.

2 4   **King John of England** (*1166*), named for his uncle by his mother and father, Queen Eleanor and King Henry II.

2 5   **Princess Alexandra, Mrs Angus Ogilvy** (*1936*), first cousin of Elizabeth II.

2 6   **Frederick II** (*1154*), future Holy Roman Emperor and the baby born in a tent erected by his 40-plus mother to prove that she had given birth.

2 7   **Anne de Mortimer, Countess of Cambridge** (*1390*), the mother of Richard Plantagenet, 3rd Duke of York and the grandmother of King Richard III. As it's likely that King Edward IV was not fathered by her son, it's unlikely that she was that King's grandmother!

2 8   **George FitzRoy, 1st Duke of Northumberland** (*1665*), third and youngest illegitimate son of Charles II by mistress Barbara Palmer.

2 9   **Savannah Phillips** (*2010*), daughter of Peter and Autumn Phillips, and Elizabeth II's first great grandchild.

3 0   **Roman Emperor Titus** (*39 AD*), completed the Coliseum in Rome and had a controversial relationship with the Jewish Queen of Judea, Berenice, who was 11 years his senior.

3 1   **Bonnie Prince Charlie** (*1720*), the Jacobite 'Young Pretender' to the British throne.

Printed in Great Britain
by Amazon.co.uk, Ltd.,
Marston Gate.